Y0-BYU-728

Taming THE Squid

Organizational Sustainability

Surviving the 21st Century

DRAFT

FIRST EDITION

Cover design by Chris Ong

Peterson, Erik W. (Erik Wayne), 1963 –

Includes bibliographical references.
ISBN 978-0-9770217-1-0

Contents

To the love of my life and my two precious daughters.
Thank you for your longsuffering patience,
grace and the love you have shown me.

Introduction

It's been said that if you aim at nothing you'll hit it every time – true in life and certainly true for people in a business organization. I have worked for various organizations and companies over 20 plus years, both private and public, prior to owning my own. In each organization it always seemed as if we were attempting to tame, and ride, a 40 ton squid. Not only could we not find the right kind of saddle, every time we were able to get one foot in the stirrup, one of the many tentacles always seemed to break loose and have one of my other business associates around the neck choking the life out of him. His terrible cry to the rest of the team would cause us to turn loose of the dangling arm we were assigned to, as we scurried over to try and rescue our ailing comrade. While all of our intentions were good, the tentacle we turned loose of was now unattended and creating yet another skirmish. In the end, it not only seemed we had failed to tame the organizational squid, but now he was in control of our organizational compass. You get the picture.

While there are a lot of great books out there (and I mean this) on leadership and management, motivation and "best practices," I've never found a book which distilled ideas by top-notch executives and consultants into a few short, simple chapters that provide clear, cogent, perspectives, with 'how to' applications written by someone who has been "in the trenches." I am not presuming to have accomplished that, but it was my intention.

Hopefully, this is not just another book that you will relegate to your bookshelf along with your collection of trophy reads, but rather an easy reference manual that you can use on a day-to-day basis, with applications that can easily be implemented. I intend for this to be a nice, short, simple field guide that you could turn to at a moment's notice to get that cold, refreshing splash of reality that says, "Oh, yeah, this doesn't have to be that complicated."

Upon reading this book, my desire is that you will be:

1. Encouraged – to take what you have learned and transform your organization into a healthy, vibrant, joyful, functional and efficient place to work. Lofty, but do-able!

2. Equipped – with a state of the art "dashboard" of practical organizational models that can be used to manage your organization, tools to create an organizational roadmap, and simple evaluation forms that will aid you in tracking the pulse of your people, your processes and your products. Combined, these tools form the organizational compass that will not only get you where you're going, but help you enjoy the journey the entire way.

3. Inspired – to teach and mentor others who will someday take your job and do it better than you did because they were trained by the best, i.e., you!

When it comes to complicated accounting, the complex nuances of running a publicly traded company, or the intricate details of filing an S.E.C. report, I have nothing to offer. I have never been a CEO of a Fortune 500 company and am very well aware that the view from 500 feet is very different from ground zero.

Before we get into the "maps, compass and hiking," I want to clarify one more thing; there is a dramatic difference between those who take hikes and those who climb Mt. Everest. I will not pretend or imply that I have Mt. Everest expertise when addressing the following subjects in this book. I will rather default to the lessons I have learned from great books and years of experience in managing people, creating processes and delivering products. On these subjects, I have a good bit of experience and knowledge, primarily from the mistakes I've made along the way. I hope this book will be helpful to you who deal in the three areas that will be addressed in this book; namely, people, processes and products.

Changing organizational culture is hard work and takes great effort and commitment. If you're looking for a quick fix, a magic wand or a simple pill, this book is probably not for you. If you're looking for practical models, tools and evaluations that can help you sustain your organization, then grab your backpack and let's take a hike, or as I call it, an "expedition" to the summit of Organizational Sustainability. See you at the top!

Prelude

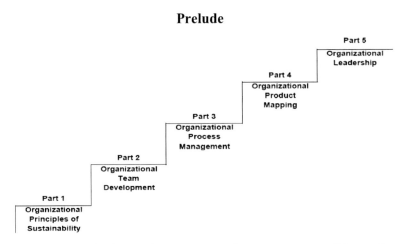

Let's look at where we're going on our expedition. In each part of the book I will be introducing a model for assessing various component parts of an organization. When you see the word "organization," I would ask you to think; people, processes and products.

Part 1 introduces the Organizational Sustainability model through which we view and evaluate the *organization*; that is, the people, the processes and the products as a whole.

Part 2 details the Organizational Team Development model based on Patrick Lencioni's book *The Five Dysfunctions of a Team*. This model is used to view and evaluate the *people*, or the teams, within your organization.

Part 3 describes the Organizational Process Management model used to view and evaluate the *processes* within your organization.

Part 4 details the Organizational Product Mapping tool used to evaluate and create a "roadmap" for the *products* that your organization produces.

Lastly, Part 5 looks at *leadership,* providing, perhaps, a different perspective from other traditional approaches to leadership.

Throughout the book you'll also notice the term "dashboard" being used. When I speak of the dashboard, my hope is that you will actually think of a dashboard as pictured below. It is simply a graphic representation of the evaluation results gathered using our company's online organizational evaluation engine. Notice that each dial represents a part of the book.

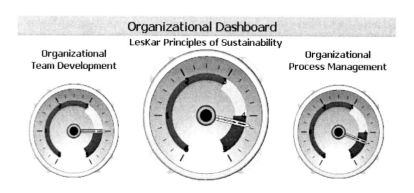

This diagram shows the overall relationship of the various concepts that will be developed in each section of the book.

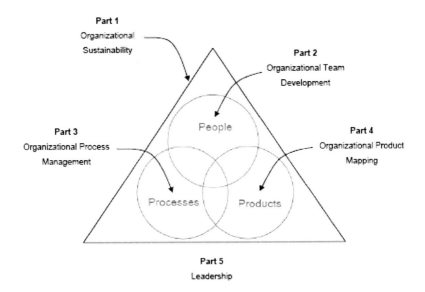

Enjoy the read!

Part 1

The Organization

Every organization – not just business – needs one core competence: innovation.

- Peter Drucker

CHAPTER ONE

What Is Organizational Sustainability?

or-gan-i-za-tion-al sus-tain-a-bil-ity

- description

1. *the ability for a group of persons organized for some end of work, to endure change and innovation (from both internal and external forces) and still endeavor through their own peculiar processes to deliver their specific products*

To improve is to change, to be perfect is to change often.

- Winston Churchill

There are a few reasons I chose to write about organizational sustainability. First, because it's wise to pay close attention to cultural trends; whether government, business, society, school, church, sports or any other norms that are shaping a society – that is, if you have a genuine interest in playing a part in how they are being shaped. If you're just along for the ride it doesn't matter. Secondly, because it's what the gurus in the field of business are talking about. And third, because it really does define what the book is all about.

As I see it, all organizations have three component parts – people, processes and products. If you are going to effectively keep an organization working in *harmony* and at the same time be *competitive* and *healthy (i.e. profitable)*, you must have an evaluation model for each part of the organization. You must have a way of *frequently* checking the "vitals" of the organization to make sure it's healthy, the same way a doctor checks blood pressure, pulse and temperature to assess the overall health of a person. To use another comparison, all understand that if one team member is not pulling his or her load, the overall success of the climb to the summit will be hindered. And as is true on a hike or expedition, so it is in business: when one person or part of an organization is slacking, the overall organization is not operating at 100%.

Now, that little tidbit of information is not revolutionary to any of you reading this book, but I want to expand on that thought for just a moment. The members of an expedition team are intrinsically motivated to make it to the summit. The same is true when taking even a short hike. Each person in the party is there because he or she wants to be – some for the shear enjoyment, some for camaraderie, and others perhaps, for the overall sense of accomplishment. Their personal motivations enhance the overall success of the group. Our goal as business owners, leaders, managers or directors is to create a culture where the same thing can happen. We need to encourage and inspire people in our organization to accomplish a given assignment or list of tasks that will benefit the organization as a whole. To do that we must lead, first by example. We'll talk specifically about leadership in Part 5 of the book.

So how do you *frequently* check the vitals of an organization? We do it once a month using what we have coined the "LesKar Principles of Sustainability." It's our Organizational Sustainability model – a sort of "dashboard" of gauges giving us information which acts as our organizational compass! Throughout my business career, I've enjoyed reading great books on management, leadership, personal growth, and project controls by some of the best authors. What I have learned, and am still learning, is that in order to maintain a healthy organization, company, team, or individual, one must be *diligent* about frequently checking their vitals. The leader must be able to see that the expedition team is still heading in the right direction, that everyone's temperature, pulse and blood pressure are still good. This is best accomplished by having a specified evaluation scheme that can be looked at on a monthly, weekly or daily basis that will remind you to challenge every facet of your organization as a whole – while at the same time challenging you as an individual leader.

The LesKar Principles of Sustainability model provides seven guiding principles that we use in an effort to have a sustainable organization. The frequency of evaluation depends on the health of the organization, but my recommendation is no less than once a month. The model looks like this:

I will explain each component of the LesKar model and how it works, why it is important and how it can be easily implemented in the next couple of chapters. In Part 2 through Part 4 of this book we will look at evaluation models applied specifically to the overall organization, the people, the processes and the products.

Before we move on, let's review the definition of Organizational Sustainability. Since we're talking about organizations, we're talking about groups of individuals organized for some specific end of work in mind. A sustainable organization, when challenged by change, can endure. Whether the change is brought on by innovation, through internal organizational pressures or some other type of external forces – perhaps personal, cultural or even global – individuals in healthy organizations still are able to collectively perform their own peculiar set of processes necessary to deliver their specific products.

Leaders who hope to have this level of organizational health must be able to check the organization's vitals. They must have a way to hear from their people in an effective manner that will cultivate healthy accountability; that will allow them to actually become part of the innovative change process that will ensure an organization's success in the 21st Century. William Pollard, in his book *The Soul of the Firm,* exhorted his readers in saying, "Only people, not machines, can respond to the unexpected and surprise the customer with extraordinary performance. Only people can serve; only people can lead; only people can innovate and create; only people can love and hate." [1]

Over the past 40 years, our culture has adopted the idea that only executives know how to innovate; only people with a Masters degree can have good ideas; only those in upper level management can play a part in organizational change. In addition, from what I have observed, organizations are terrified of transparency because with transparency comes accountability. And accountability cries out for change.

In our crazed culture of self-esteem, "wellness" and political correctness, organizations across this country have made what I believe to be futile attempts to address declining productivity, falling profits and decreasing market share. They have been anesthetized by *entitlement* thinking and often have failed to address the real problem – the need to change the internal culture of the organization. When people sense they are truly valued and heard, and that the leadership values their work for something other than just a bottom line buck, they will become more than just employees. Employees will transform and become the very fabric of the organization. Pollard further said, "It is not just what we are doing, but what we are becoming in the process that gives us our distinct value and is uniquely human." [2] And I would add that when individuals know that you are taking a

---

[1] C. William Pollard, *The Soul of The Firm* (Grand Rapids: Zondervan Publishing House, 1996), 26.
[2] *Ibid.*

genuine interest in their work and in their personal lives, they will perform beyond your expectations. In his book *Inside Drucker's Brain*, Jeffrey Krames quotes Jim Collins as saying that legendary businessman Peter Drucker was "infused with his humanity, and above all [had]...a very, very deep compassion for the individual."[3]

In the next chapter we'll take a closer look at what I believe to be part of the solution to the need for cultural change in the organization.

---

[3] Jeffrey A. Krames, *Inside Drucker's Brain*, (New York: Penguin Group), 130.

CHAPTER TWO

Changing Internal Culture

LesKar Principles of Sustainability

There is nothing wrong with change, if it is in the right direction.

- Winston Churchi.

Watering the Cultural Soil

If our organizations are going to stand the test of time amid the challenges that await us in the 21st century, we must begin to cultivate and water the internal organizational soil to allow individuals to be intrinsically motivated. We certainly must have a clear vision, a cogent plan and effective means, but we must also have courageously dedicated people who are not afraid of accountability. People are not *only* extrinsically motivated through compensation, but also intrinsically motivated by the virtue of work itself. To which you may reply, "Okay, so how do we do that?"

First, and above all else, it takes courageous leadership. Second, it takes leaders who will tirelessly persevere and who relentlessly encourage others. And third, as we learned in Chapter 1, it takes leaders who are "infused" with their people and, who like Drucker, "above all...[have] a very, very deep compassion for the individual."

Before we move to the practical "how to" in just a few pages, let's look back in history at a few leaders who faced far greater challenges and opposition than we could ever imagine. These men were not only successful in enduring their trials, they were also able to encourage and sustain those around them.

I have included the quotes below to serve as both an illustration and an encouragement to those of you who are leaders.

It takes courage to lead. It takes courage to change. And it takes courage to risk.

Standing all of 5'-7", Sir Winston Churchill has gone down as one of the greatest leaders of the 20th century. If anyone understood "Organizational Sustainability" – while he might not have called it that at the time – it was Mr. Churchill. Below are some excerpts taken from some of his most famous speeches while serving as Prime Minister of the United Kingdom before, during and after World War II:

I have nothing to offer, but blood, toil, tears and sweat… It is victory, victory at all costs, victory in spite of all terror, victory, however long and hard the road may be; for without victory, there is no survival…we shall never surrender" he warned in an especially bleak radio address. "Not only great dangers, but many more misfortunes, many shortcomings, many mistakes, many disappointments will surely be our lot. Death and sorrow will be companions of our journey, constancy and valor our only shield… We must be united, we must be undaunted. We must be inflexible… never give in, never give in, never, never, never, never-in nothing, great or small, large or petty - never give in except to convictions of honour and good sense. Never yield to force; never yield to the apparently overwhelming might of the enemy."[4]

---

[4] Taken from various speeches made available on The Churchill Center website; http://www.winstonchurchill.org

Needless to say, Great Britain was victorious. And I would argue they were victorious simply because one man had the courage to step out and encourage his people to stand with him. And if your organization or my organization is going to survive in this 21st century, we must be motivated by something other than monetary compensation and entitlements.

I am keenly aware that our survival is not about life or death in the physical sense, but it *is* about surviving as an organization. Here's another:

Consistently ranked by scholars as one of the greatest American Presidents, Theodore Roosevelt knew how to encourage people. Having successfully commanded a volunteer regiment called the "Rough Riders" during the Spanish American War, serving as the Governor of New York, Vice President of the United States, 26th President of the United States and the first American to ever receive the Nobel Peace Prize, Mr. Roosevelt knew the importance of intrinsically motivating and encouraging his followers. In an excerpt from a speech titled "Citizenship in a Republic," delivered at the University of Paris on April 23, 1910, Mr. Roosevelt promised only hardship and unwavering resolve for those who endeavor to embark on true greatness:

It is not the critic who counts; not the man who points out how the strong man stumbles, or where the doer of deeds could have done them better. The credit belongs to the man who is actually in the arena, whose face is marred by dust and sweat and blood; who strives valiantly; who errs, who comes short again and again, because there is no effort without error and shortcoming; but who does actually strive to do the deeds; who knows great enthusiasms, the great devotions; who spends himself in a worthy cause; who at the best knows in the end the triumph of high achievement, and who at the worst, if he fails, at least fails while daring greatly, so that his place shall never be with those cold and timid souls who neither know victory nor defeat... We must ever remember that no keenness and subtleness of intellect, no polish, no cleverness, in any way make up for the lack of the great solid qualities. Self-restraint, self-mastery, common sense, the power of accepting individual responsibility and yet of acting in conjunction with others, courage and resolution - these are the qualities which mark a masterful people. Without them no people can control itself, or save itself from being controlled from the outside.

These were two great leaders encouraging their audience through intrinsic motivation – not wellness, not entitlements, not free healthcare, not free education, not free childcare, not a guaranteed retirement, not anything other than "blood, toil, tears and sweat."

How about President Abraham Lincoln? Arguably one of the greatest Presidents who gave one of the greatest speeches ever delivered on American soil during the American Civil War. In similar form to the two previous excerpts you have read, Mr. Lincoln encourages his audience in Gettysburg to *"give the same measure [death]...to the great task remaining before [them]" -- that we here highly resolve that these dead shall not have died in vain -- that this nation, under God, shall have a new birth of freedom -- and that government of the people, by the people, for the people, shall not perish from the earth.*

General George Washington on December 24, 1776, facing insurmountable odds on the eve of their attack on Trenton, mustered freezing cold men who had left their families, fought for over two years and who were starving. Washington scribbled on scraps of paper, *"Victory or Death,"* and delivered them to his bedraggled troops along with the words, *"These are the times that try men's souls"*; taken from Thomas Paine's essay, "The Crisis," written only a few days before.

These four great leaders were able to empower their followers through encouragement, and as a result, change their culture and sustain their "organization." If it can be done at a national level during crisis, do I dare suggest that we should be able to do the same within the walls of our own companies? Oh, I can already hear a handful of readers saying, "Come on, those were life or death situations! Do you really expect me to be able to motivate my folks to attack their monthly reports or daily activities with the same valor as those in World War II or the Civil War?"

Well, to be totally honest with you – no! That is unless they are trained and encouraged in such a way. And, no, I do not expect your staff to show up day after day ready to fight for your company and for their jobs as if it were life or death. But, that *is* the essence of Organizational Sustainability; encouraging, challenging, motivating and holding each other accountable as individuals to take personal responsibility for actions, innovation and change, cultivating a culture of enthusiasm and high achievement, a culture of accountability and a culture where individuals "spend themselves in a worthy cause" – both in and outside the organization.

A Proposed First Step

The way I see it, over the past thirty to forty years, our culture has slowly allowed a crust of entitlement clay to be placed over the fertile soil of individual hearts. The result: complacency, a stifling of encouragement and intrinsic motivation, or even a lack of desire for individuals to engage in their jobs, communities, and, sadly enough, even their own personal lives. It's as if we've drifted lazily into a pool of despondency where individuals and even entire organizations prefer entitlement or government programs over personal responsibility and accountability.

Patrick Lencioni, in his book *The Three Signs of a Miserable Job*, succinctly states that a manager, and I might add owner, executive, V.P. or anyone else, can have a profound impact on employees. "By helping people find fulfillment in their work, and helping them succeed in whatever they're doing, a manager can have a profound impact on the emotional, financial, physical, and spiritual health of workers and their families. They can also create an environment where employees do the same for their peers, giving them a sort of ministry of their own. All of which is nothing short of a gift from God."[5]

With that, I would like to offer a first step in cultivating Organizational Sustainability; creating a company creed. I am a big proponent of mission statements, but a mission statement only

---

[5] Patrick Lencioni, *Three Signs of a Miserable Job*(San Francisco, Josey Bass, 2007), 253

provides the sense of direction for the organization and states the organization's overall goals. A creed goes much deeper than that. A creed offers a cogent, authoritative, formulated statement of an organization's belief. It appeals to the intrinsic values of an individual, and if you are going to – in the words of Jim Collins – get the right people on the bus, then you had better make certain prospective team members have the same or a very similar intrinsic motivation for achieving what the organization is trying to accomplish. Here is our company creed:

LesKar Creed

In an effort to stay healthy and competitive as both an individual and organization, we must be willing to cultivate daily a culture of change and innovation in our personal life and within our organization – always aiming for perfection. We will make every effort to remove complacency and always strive to learn by carefully questioning, diligently searching, and honestly pursuing the advice of those who have gone before us. Additionally, we will seek advice from those who model genuine moral uprightness in their respective field. We then must take what we have learned and sow, or share that knowledge with our peers and carefully administer and grow that into our own personal life and the life of the organization. We must commit to not just knowing, but also embracing, that we will be accountable to our peers, as well as those who have been placed in authority over us. And lastly, we must commit to mentoring those around us and those we have been given responsibility over, as we understand and look forward to the day when they will be able to effectively perform the job that we have been given – only better.

Notice the words "we" and "us" mentioned fourteen times. No secret here that "we" are emphasizing *individual responsibility, accountability* and *team* in maintaining Organizational Sustainability. Those who are placed in authority then become a "leader among equals," and not oppressive dictators.

Take note of that last statement please: "a leader among equals." Your people will begin to trust and follow you when they recognize humility– and boy, is that a hard character trait to model – especially for a leader! I might also add that our creed is written on a fabric made of a genuine love for people.

At this juncture in the book, I think I know what some of you might be thinking: "So, you expect me to be able to change the internal culture of my organization by giving some heroic speeches and coming up with a creed?" The simple answer to that question is "no." The creed is only a first step. Read on to the end of this section and you'll see how it ties together. In the next chapter you will learn the practical side of Organizational Sustainability, how it works and how it can easily be implemented.

CHAPTER THREE

How It Works

LesKar Principles of Sustainability

Knowing is not enough, we must apply. Willing is not enough, we must do.

- *Johann von Goethe*

I believe it was Bruce Shelley who said, "The mother of all learning is repetition." To go a step further, I would then have to say, "The father of execution is diligence." If there is one secret to successful change in an organization it would have to be intentional diligence; a persistent, purposeful, earnest effort to accomplish what you set out to do. I'm sure you have all heard, "The road to hell is paved with good intentions." Simply hoping your organization is going to change isn't good enough. I've heard it said that wishful thinking is like "leaning on a shovel and praying for a hole." In other words, changing your organization is going to take effort.

Known as a man of few words and even nicknamed "Silent Cal," Calvin Coolidge, the 30th President of the United States, penned perhaps the most profound words ever written on staying persistent to a cause:

Nothing in the world can take the place of Persistence. Talent will not; nothing is more common than unsuccessful men with talent.
Genius will not; unrewarded genius is almost a proverb.
Education will not; the world is full of educated derelicts.
Persistence and determination alone are omnipotent.

I assume those of you who are taking the time to read this book possess some semblance of a persistent character. But whether you do or not, I want to encourage you to stay the course in implementing the LesKar Principles of Sustainability.

It works like this: just like any other good or bad habit, healthy practices are formed by diligent repetition. Therefore, if you desire your people to embrace these new principles, it will take time and diligence; but I can assure you, the time and effort it does take will be well worth it. Perhaps for the first time, your people will be given an opportunity to speak. And it may be the first time you have ever heard from your people what they think of the organization as a whole.

Let's look closely at each of the seven steps in the LesKar guiding principles.

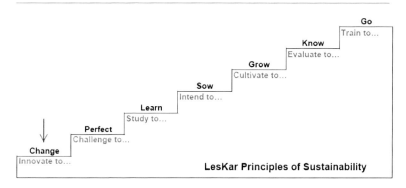

Innovate to Change

Why do you suppose we have made change and innovation the first step of our Sustainability Model? Because all of those who are counted among the ranks of greatness throughout history were committed to change. I might also clarify, this does not imply changing for change's sake. We mean change for the sake of progress and improvement. C.S. Lewis astutely observed, "We all want progress. But progress means getting nearer to the place where you want to be. And if you have taken a wrong turning, then to go forward does not get you any nearer. If you are on the wrong road, progress means doing an about-turn and walking back to the right road; and in that case the man who turns back soonest is the most progressive man."[6] So if we want to be "the most" progressive company, we must approach each day with the attitude that we are committed to change – individually and organizationally—no matter where such progress takes us in the short term.

---

[6] C.S. Lewis, *Mere Christianity* (New York: Macmillan, 1952), 36.

Peter Drucker saw business as "society's change agent." He also said, "The seemingly most successful business of today is a sham and a failure if it does not create its own and different tomorrow. It must innovate and re-create its products or services but equally the enterprise itself."[7]

Gary Hamel, in his book *The Future of Management,* said, "In a world where strategy life cycles are shrinking, innovation is the only way a company can renew its lease on success. It's also the only way it can survive in a world of bare-knuckled competition."[8] He goes on to say that "innovation is everyone's job.[9]"

I want to emphasize that everyone needs to be on board with changing, both individually and organizationally, but this is not a free-for-all to tear apart the organization. We have to start with ourselves!

---

[7] Jeffrey A. Krames, *Inside Drucker's Brain*, (New York: Penguin Group, 2008), 159.
[8] Gary Hamel with Bill Breen, *The Future of Management,* (Massachusetts: Harvard Business School Publishing, 2007), 48.
[9] *Ibid.*, 50.

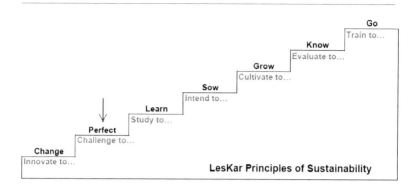

LesKar Principles of Sustainability

Challenge to Perfect

Okay, so we have a good reason to embrace change. But what are we embracing change for? Remember, we are in pursuit of *perfection*. We are *not* trying to become perfectionists! Perfectionists are those who can make everyone's life miserable in demanding that everything be done in a certain way. Paper clips just so, their ideas are the only good ones, everyone's desk needs to look like it just rolled off the showroom floor, et al. What I am talking about is raising the bar on performance, on processes, on products and on individual behavior.

Jeffrey K. Liker, in his masterpiece *The Toyota Way*,[10] goes into extensive detail about Toyota's "4 P" model. Their model challenges their people in all aspects of the organization; the philosophy, the processes, the people and problem solving.

In our company, we challenge all aspects of the organization; the different markets that we can penetrate, the

---

[10] Jeffrey K. Liker, *The Toyota Way,* (New York: McGraw-Hill, 2004)

processes we go through, the font we use on our meeting minutes, the format and style of the reports we send to our clients. We challenge one another to encourage the people we work with, learn the names of their family, ask what their hobbies are, and so on. We are all striving for perfection. There's always room for improvement at every level of the organization and even within everyone's personal life. Remember, as has been said, no one is perfect, that's why pencils have erasers! But, they have erasers   to correct the mistakes that have been made – not leave them.

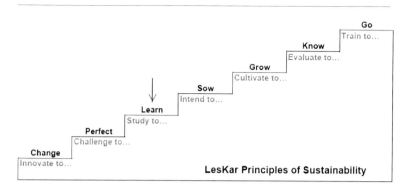

LesKar Principles of Sustainability

Study to Learn

You finally got the degree, the job, the position, the sale, whatever it may be. Well, sorry to be the one to break the news, but you're not done learning. You have probably heard it said that "Readers are leaders and leaders are readers," and I couldn't agree more. If you're not a reader, take a deep breath and know that you are in good company. You can still learn by surrounding yourself with folks who are, and by learning the art of listening. Listen and learn.

If you are a reader, you should still learn the art of listening. Seek advice of those who have held or are holding similar positions. Commit as an individual and organization to "knowledge sharing." In our small company, we have what we call "Lessons Learned" sessions where we share what mistakes and successes we've had along the way. Write them down and share them, however big or small they may be.

As we're almost half way up the steps, I think this is a good time for a break and a "real life" short story. I'll never forget meeting Harvey Mackay in his office almost 20 years ago. I was in Minneapolis on a business trip and had just read his best selling book *Swim with the Sharks Without Being Eaten Alive,* a book that I still reference frequently. I thought, "What the heck! I know Harvey lives and works here, so I think I'll just drop by his office and see if he's in. What are the chances: New York Times best selling author, one of the most sought after public speakers and owner and president of a multi- million dollar paper company?"

I got a phone book, looked up the address and drove to his office, walked in, introduced myself to the receptionist and asked if Harvey was in. She asked who I was, and I told her. She politely asked, "Is Mr. Mackay expecting you?" I said, "No," but that I had just driven in from Wyoming and thought I'd stop by. To keep this short, the receptionist smiled, got up from her chair and went in to Mr. Mackay's office. She came out and said, "Right this way, sir." I went into his office, he greeted me with a handshake and a big smile, and we sat and talked for about 20 minutes.

I cannot recall every word of the conversation, but I can say that he exuded kindness and excitement. After our brief encounter, he grabbed one of his books from off the floor; they were stacked all over his office. He picked up a pen and wrote on the inside leaf, stood up, handed me the book and encouraged me on my way. I walked out somewhat numb at what had just happened, got back into my car and opened the cover of the book. This is what he had written:

"Dear Erik,
Knowledge does not become power until it is used! Dive in!
Harvey Mackay

I took that to mean "you gotta share it" – and still do!

If you are a reader, then you have a responsibility to share that information. That way others are learning along with you. Professor and author Howard Hendricks said, "You cannot impart what you do not possess." Learning so you can share with others goes hand-in-hand with our last guiding principle, "Train to Go" that we'll get to in a few pages. But the message is still clear:

Listen >>> Learn >>> Live >>> Leave!

One way to encourage continual learning is by assigning a book to your project teams, executive staff or certain departments. Have them schedule a short meeting each week or every other week to discuss and share what they have learned. If you had them meet every other week for 26 weeks and asked them to read just two chapters between each meeting, that would get them through 52 chapters. How many books can you think of with 52 chapters? The bottom line is your people could get through at least two books a year. Not to mention, it could build camaraderie, trust and may even allow them an opportunity to introduce something new into the organization that would make it better. Commit to learning!

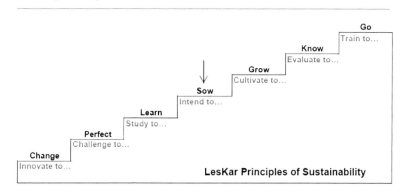

Intend to Sow

So you're committed to changing. You're committed to striving for perfection and even challenging your team to read a book together. The next step would appear to be an easy one, and it can be, but often times it isn't. Your goal now will be for your people to intentionally sow, or "apply" what they are experiencing into the organization. It's one thing to learn something new, and an entirely different thing to get them to apply it.

We are creatures of habit, and old habits die hard – but they do die. This is where the true leader begins to search for what C.J. Mahaney, in his book *Humility,* calls, "Identifying evidences of grace in others." He says, "…only those who are humble can consistently identify evidences of grace in others who need adjustment."[11] When I first read that, I thought, "That sounds too touchy feely for me." But as I kept reading, I really began to understand what he was saying. In other words, look for ways to

---

[11] C.J. Mahaney, *Humility; True Greatness,* (Colorado: Multnomah Books, 2005), 100.

encourage those who have embraced, even in the smallest ways, the changes you are making. Understand that we are *all* proud and that when your folks embrace change, they are actually letting go of the way *they* used to do things. And that, be it ever so small, is an opportunity for you to encourage change behavior.

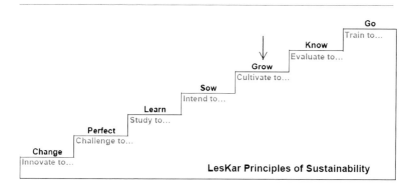

LesKar Principles of Sustainability

Cultivate to Grow

Cultivating growth is when others begin to encourage one another in what they are doing as a result of introducing the LesKar Principles of Sustainability. Look for opportunities to encourage those who are cultivating the group or department, and who are a taking a leadership role in implementing Organizational Sustainability Principles. By carefully watching, you will be able to identify future leaders. They're the ones who are not just satisfied with applying what they have learned in their own life, but also encourage others around them. Go out of your way to acknowledge what you have observed. These folks will become the future leaders and champions of your organization!

Actively *search* for opportunities to encourage folks who are cultivating these principles in the work place. I'm not talking about flattery: flattery encourages an individual in bad behavior. Flattery is *not* genuine and people can smell it from a mile away. I'm talking about genuine, honest to goodness encouragement. Perhaps you stop someone after a meeting and say something like,

"Hey, Ken, I just wanted to thank you for sharing in the meeting with Laura how you have changed your reports to include so and so…" You get the picture. Be intentional about encouraging those who are cultivating change in your organization.

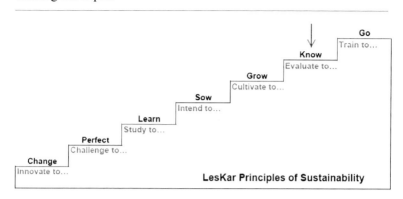

Evaluate to Know

I believe proper accountability is the biggest shortcoming in almost every organization that I have either worked or consulted for, and for that reason, this is the most powerful tool in the LesKar Principles of Sustainability. No fancy software is required: no training is needed.

Organizations usually do have a clear "Reporting Structure," but hardly ever do you see peer-to-peer evaluation. This lets people *know* that accountability is everyone's responsibility. What I mean by that is, organizations seldom take the time to sit down with co-workers to evaluate their peers laterally in the organization, and then have those evaluations go to their immediate supervisors, who in turn report what their people are saying to their supervisor. We call this "Leapfrog Accountability."

Leapfrog Accountability works like this: Let's say we have an organization; we'll call it Beacon Enterprises. Let's say

Beacon has a division president who has two vice presidents that report to him. Each V.P. has two directors under him, and each director has four managers under him. Let's say Beacon Enterprises decides to conduct an Organizational Management Evaluation every other month. Every VP, director and manager is required to fill out the evaluation form. It's a simple one page form made up of three categories with five questions under each category that are to be rated on a scale from 1 – 5. There is a space at the bottom of the page that allows the person evaluating to write comments for every question that receives a score of 3 or less, because if it's not rated a 4 or 5, then the person needs to know why and how he can make it better.

Now, let's say that we have a director for Beacon Enterprises who isn't being trustworthy, isn't communicating well and is not overly committed to being real honest with his team. He's rude, crude and condescending to all of the managers, and, oh, by the way, he's been known to fire anyone who crosses or questions him. We'll call him Mr. Snotty Pants. Needless to say, his managers' "job satisfaction rating" is in the tubes; not because the managers don't like what they're doing; they don't like who their doing it for – and they NEVER hear a word of encouragement from the V.P. above them. Sound familiar?

Under the current Beacon Enterprise model, they only do *annual* Performance Evaluations that are conducted by the immediate supervisors over each department. The result: turnover is through the roof at Beacon Enterprises, and most everyone that works there is unhappy.

What if Beacon Enterprises implemented the Leapfrog Accountability model into their organization? Suppose Mr. Snotty Pants received a score of 2 or 1 from three of his subordinates, who also noted on the evaluation something to the effect: "*Mr. Snotty Pants is rude. He treats people like they are second rate citizens and never has a good thing to say about anyone and I don't trust him.*" Don't forget, in the Leapfrog Accountability model, Mr. Snotty Pants has to share his four managers' evaluations with *his* V.P., and perhaps most importantly, he has to hear from his managers what he has to report.

In the above scenario, we only heard from four line managers reporting to one director on only one question of a 20 question evaluation. Just imagine for a moment what feedback you could get if you heard from sixteen line managers reporting to four directors who were all reporting their results to their V.P. Might I suggest you would begin to see real change and thorough transparency? Understand this is not some kind of "tattle tale" evaluation that only has to do with pointing out the supervisors' faults. This is an evaluation form that challenges the sustainability principles, the team and the processes.

I can already hear what some of the V.P.'s, the Division Presidents and CEO's are thinking; "We simply don't have time for that, and it would take away from what we need to stay focused on." It would take time initially, but in the end it would save time, cut turnover and improve performance. In a sense, it would create transparent accountability that would foster "community" and not stale "bureaucracy." Perhaps most importantly, it fosters innovation and change that keep the organization profitable.

If you will allow me, I would like to share a rather lengthy quote from Gary Hamel, author of *The Future of Management*, on the difference between a bureaucracy and a community: *"Hierarchies are very good at aggregating effort, at coordinating activities of many people with widely varying roles. But they're not very good at mobilizing effort, at inspiring people to go above and beyond. When it comes to mobilizing human capability, communities outperform bureaucracies. This is true for several reasons. In a bureaucracy, the basis for exchange is contractual – you get paid for doing what is assigned to you. In a community, exchange is voluntary – you give your labor in return for the chance to make a difference, or exercise your talents. In a bureaucracy you are a factor of production. In a community you are a partner in a cause. In a bureaucracy, "loyalty" is a product of economic dependency. In a community, dedication and commitment are based on one's affiliation with the group's aims and goals. When it comes to supervision and control, bureaucracies rely on multiple layers of management and a web of policies and rules. Communities, by contrast, depend on norms, values, and gentle prodding of one's peers. Individual contributions tend to be circumscribed in a bureaucracy...In a community, capability and disposition are more important than credentials and job descriptions in determining who does what. And where the rewards offered by a bureaucracy are mostly financial, in a community they're mostly emotional. When compared with bureaucracies, communities tend to be under managed. That, more than anything else, is why they are amplifiers of human capability.*[12]

I am not suggesting, and I don't believe Gary Hamel is either, that we obliterate organizational hierarchy or create some form of a classless organizational society where everyone earns the same pay with no direct accountability. That's absurd! Karl Marx talked about it: Lenin tried it and failed; his successor Stalin wasn't any more successful. The "trendy" term of today is "a flat organization" where everyone's paid the same. That is not what I'm talking about.

I'm talking about effective leadership; leadership that fosters community, aggregates effort, effectively coordinates people and successfully accomplishes the activities that are necessary in achieving an end goal. And leadership, by definition, requires authority, welcomes responsibility and embraces open and honest accountability.

---

[12] Gary Hamel with Bill Breen, *The Future of Management,* (Massachusetts: Harvard Business School Publishing, 2007), 62.

I'm also suggesting that your people be given an opportunity to be heard and exercise their talents to become part of an organizational family – and families *have* a hierarchy of leadership. When led effectively with a genuine respect for each member, organizations experience a synergy that creates community, which in turn leads to sustainability. And how do you foster this type of effective leadership? By creating a "dashboard" that monitors the vitals of your organization based on honest and frequent evaluations.

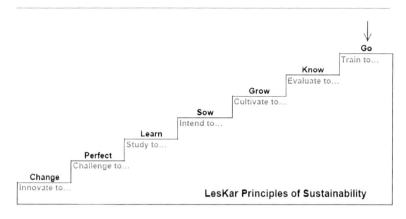

LesKar Principles of Sustainability

Train to Go

Last and certainly not least on our LesKar Principles of Sustainability model is "Go." We've talked about *change* and becoming an organization that embraces change and creates an environment that fosters innovation. We've learned about raising the bar and striving for *perfection*. We've stressed the importance of getting your folks involved in *learning*, reading something together and/or studying. We then moved on to *applying* what they learn into their own work discipline and the need to encourage them when you see this happening. From there we learned the importance of not just applying what they have learned in their own disciplines, but *growing* or *cultivating* what they have learned through knowledge sharing. And now we're just coming off of a rather long session on *evaluating* so you know you are going to be held *accountable*. The next guiding principle is *Train to Go*. So it looks like this:

Change>>>Perfect>>>Learn>>>Sow>>>Grow>>>Know>>>Go

In his book *Good to Great*, Jim Collins revealed several fascinating discoveries about organizations that were able to stand the test of time. In Chapter 6 of his book, titled "A Culture of Discipline," he highlights three particular companies which were indeed successful while under the reign of some gifted CEO's, but when they retired, the companies practically fell apart. *"Whereas the good-to-great companies had Level 5 leaders who built an enduring culture of discipline, the un-sustained comparisons had Level 4 leaders who personally disciplined the organization through sheer force."*[13]

The goal of any leader should always be to pass along what he has learned and what he is learning to either his peers or to those he has been given responsibility for. Jeffrey Krames said, "Drucker knew that leadership development was a key to a company's future...Drucker also felt that every leader had to plan for his or her successor."[14] Quoting Drucker, Krames writes, "The gravest indictment of a leader is for the organization to collapse as soon as he leaves or dies...as happens all too often in companies."[15]

---

[13] Jim Collins, *Good to Great,* (New York: HarperCollins, 2001), 130.
[14] Jeffrey A. Krames, *Inside Drucker's Brain*, (New York: Penguin Group, 2008), 134.
[15] Ibid., 134.

So how do you cultivate a culture of *training to go and reproduce?* Simple, you provide teaching opportunities. The next time you have a staff meeting, require one of your people to do a short presentation. A word of caution: standing up and presenting or teaching for some people is a terrifying experience, so be careful that you don't embarrass or just totally freak your people out. I'm sure you've all heard or read about the "Top 10 Things People Are Most Afraid of," and public speaking somehow ends up ranking above burning to death. I've actually never seen that survey, but that's what "they" say. (My wife would rank herself among those that would rather burn than speak.) All that said, it is a very scary thing for some people to do.

Another, perhaps less intimidating, method of providing teaching opportunities is through one-on-one mentorships. You can partner a person who has strength in some skill with one who is weaker. Recommend that the one who is better show the other person how a skill is done most effectively and make recommendations on how the other person might do it better. All the time you are encouraging them both in the process.

Lastly and perhaps most evidently, if you want your people to learn to teach, you, the leader, have got to be disciplined yourself in teaching them. If they aren't getting it, you're not teaching it. It's that simple.

CHAPTER FOUR

How Do You Implement Them?

LesKar Principles of Sustainability

Implementation begets execution.

In changing the culture of an organization, I believe it's important to exercise the "slower is better than faster" approach. The worst thing you can do is overload your team with a bunch of new ideas, procedures or evaluations that can end up stifling the innovative change process. As Krames observed, "The challenge is to establish and foster a culture that encourages innovative decision making throughout the ranks, but at the same time permits the company to go on operating at 100 percent while the changes are taking place."[16]

There are several ways and many ideas out there, but the single greatest influence on your people will be for *you* to model what you are trying to do. So in the spirit of "practicing what you preach" and modeling the LesKar Principles of Sustainability Model, I would recommend the following:

First, assign a book that you think would be beneficial to the entire group. I might recommend *Taming the Squid* by Erik W. Peterson. You then would be modeling *change*. Second, challenge them by stating that *you* recognize your organization isn't as good as it could be and that you want to strive to have the best organization in your industry. Together you can *learn*. You can discuss the principles of the book together, do the Implementation & Study Guide together once a week or every other week, and *apply* what you are learning in your own

---

[16] Jeffrey A. Krames, *Inside Drucker's Brain*, (New York: Penguin Group, 2008), 215.

organization. Third, you then can begin to *cultivate* through encouragement what you are learning. Fourth, *know* that you are going to be held *accountable* and even tell your people that you want to be held accountable. Make sure they're seated because some of them may fall off their chairs in disbelief! And lastly, as you are discussing the book you will actually be modeling the *train to go* principle which will reproduce great employees.

One way to assure that you are making progress in implementing the LesKar Principles of Sustainability is to conduct a short evaluation. In our company, we do this about once a month using our LesKar Dashboard evaluation tool. The process is simple, which is how you want to keep all of your evaluations.

We started with simply evaluating through a series of brief questions, ranking each item on a scale of 1 to 5, and talking through them. We have now created an evaluation form that captures not only the LesKar Principles of Sustainability but also what we will be discussing in the subsequent chapters; Organizational Team Development and Organizational Process Management.

At our website, you can download our forms or take a complimentary organizational survey. The forms are not intended to act as an exhaustive organizational evaluation, but rather a high level evaluation aggregating feedback from all of the parties. We have found that we can complete a form in only a few minutes, yet they touch on the three component parts of the organization that we outlined at the beginning of the book: people, processes and products. We've just recently added another section on leadership, as we felt it necessary to take a quick 'character inventory' of not only organizational leadership as a whole, but also each individual.

And there you have it. We have discussed the LesKar Principles of Sustainability as they apply to the organization as a whole. In the next section, Part 2, we'll be looking at the *people* side of the organization; in Part 3 the Processes, in Part 4 the Products and in Part 5 Leadership.

At this time I would like to invite you to look back at Chapter 2 and read the LesKar Creed. Give some thought on how you might write a creed for your own organization or use the LesKar Creed. It will not only help you define your guiding principles as an organization, but will also provide a sense of clarity to why you do what you do.

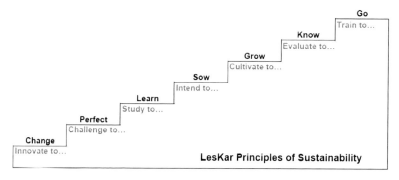

Part 2

Organizational Team Development

CHAPTER FIVE

What Is Organizational Team Development?

or-gan-i-za-tion-al team de-vel-op-ment

- description

1. *the exercise of transforming a committed group of individuals into a cohesive unit.*

To succeed as a team is to hold all of the members accountable for their expertise.

> *- Mitchell Caplan, CEO, E*Trade Group Inc.*

In Part 1 of our book we discussed Organizational Sustainability and what that looks like. We defined Organizational Sustainability as *the ability for a group of persons organized for some end of work, to endure change and innovation (from both internal and external forces) and still endeavor through their own peculiar processes to deliver their specific products.* In other words, what an organization needs to do to stay healthy.

We then went on to explain the LesKar Principles of Sustainability which acted as our model, or lens through which we look at the overall health of an organization and how to apply each of those principles.

Organizations are comprised of people, and typically those people are organized into groups or "teams." I understand that the nomenclature may change from organization to organization, so whether you call them departments, groups, cells, teams, or whatever, the same principle applies.

That said, we define Organizational Team Development as: *the exercise of transforming a committed group of individuals into a cohesive unit.*

Throughout Part 2, we will be drilling down into each of the five steps of our Organizational Team Development model. This model, adapted from Patrick Lencioni's book *The Five Dysfunctions of a Team,* looks like this:

In the next chapter we will briefly look at people and some general ground rules that must be applied if you want to change the overall attitude in your organization. Following that chapter, we will provide a model through which you can apply Organizational Team Development.

CHAPTER SIX

People Are Funny Critters

Organizational Team Model

Action springs not from thought, but from a readiness for responsibility.

- Dietrich Bonhoeffer

Described by the New York Times as "...probably the nation's most successful poet," cowboy poet Baxter Black has given us a poem that provides a glimpse into who we are as people.

People Are Funny Critters

There's apple pie bakers, And crooked book makers,
And blondes and brunetters, And birthday forgetters,
And chicken fry lovers, And blue eyed soul brothers,
And drinkers and boozers, And winners and losers,
And elephant trainers, And tireless campaigners,
And fixers and menders, And paper clip benders,
And goers and stayers, And pinochle players,
And handkerchief users, And tissue abusers,
And interstate bikers, And wilderness hikers,
And joggers and addicts, And handball fanatics,
And kissers and tellers, And friends of the fellers,
And lovers and fighters, And finger nail biters,
And mayonnaise dippers, And miracle whippers,
And newspaper readers, And drivers and speeders,
And overweight hookers, And magazine lookers,
And people with answers, And bottomless dancers,
And quivering flunkers, And basketball dunkers,
And readers and thinkers, And double scotch drinkers,
And soda straw manglers, And bar napkin stranglers,
And teasers and triers, And high rolling flyers,
And uncles and sisters, And passive resisters,
And virtuous girlies, And sillies and squirlies,
And weirdoes and sickies, And five dollar quickies,
And xylophone pickers, And popsicle lickers,
And yawners and nappers, And one handicappers,
And zippy old timers, And lunatic rhymers.
People are funny critters.

When I decided that I would divide the book into five parts, with Part 2 being on people, Black's poem immediately entered my mind. I heard it first about 35 years ago on television recited by the Dallas Cowboy fullback, Walt Garrison. For some odd reason, I have never forgotten it – perhaps because it really does capture the diversity of people we all must work with on a day-to-day basis.

Like the people that Baxter Black identifies in his poem, there are all kinds, and it's up to you to figure out how they all tick and how to use their individual talents and gifts most effectively. "Up to me?" you ask. "I thought you were going to give us some new insight into how people think or provide a new psychological break through into how teams gel?" Nope. But I will provide you a few elementary methods that have passed the test of time, that transcend gender, ethnicity and every other cultural norm that's out there.

Here they are:
1.   No whining or complaining.
2.   No gossiping.
3.   Pull your own weight.
4.   Put on a good attitude.

Let's spend a few minutes on each of these rules.

No Whining or Complaining

Why no whining or complaining? Because whiners and complainers squelch enthusiasm, and they're a drag on the team; they're like parasites. We've all worked around them and we all know at least one. Nothing is ever good enough. Nothing is ever right. Nothing is ever the way it needs to be, and on and on they go. If you have one, or even worse, more than one, sit down with them and let them know that whining and complaining will no longer be tolerated. If they have a legitimate concern, then they can bring it up, but also tell them that if they do have a concern or problem, they need to bring a solution to the table. If your organization is going to be sustainable, it must be made up of teams that are positive and encouraging. This doesn't mean that you ignore legitimate concerns or that you squash open dialogue; it simply means you will no longer allow petty whining and complaining.

No Gossiping

There's a Proverb that says, "A perverse man stirs up dissension and a gossip separates close friends." Gossip is like a cancer. If it goes unchecked, it will kill the organization. You need to instruct your team from the onset that if they've got a beef with someone, they first need to address the person one-on-one and "clear the air." If that doesn't work, they need to go to the team leader, and the two of them need to address the problem. Two critical components to addressing any personnel problem are gentleness and restoration. Often times, when confronted, we find that a gossiping individual has simply fallen into a rut, and they just need to be restored. We've all been there, and this is where the humble leader can show his true colors and lead by example.

If the gossiping individual responds in a positive way, then mission accomplished. If they continue in their gossiping behavior, then *you* as the leader need to take decisive and corrective action. Yes, that means firing! I want to emphasize that you as a leader *must* make certain that you have given that person a chance to change, provided a clear understanding of your expectations and allowed an appropriate time for the individual to make changes. Remember, lead by example and treat that person *precisely* the way you would want to be treated in the same situation.

Your actions, throughout the process and regardless of the outcome, will set the tone for the rest of the team in moving forward.

Pull Your Own Weight

There's another Proverb that says, "One who is slack in his work is brother to one who destroys." If you're going to have a successful team everyone must pull his own weight. If you've got a "slacker" on the team, you need to encourage him to pick it up. Remember in Chapter 1 we used the illustration of being on an expedition. Well, if everyone is carrying their own load, then we have no problems. When just one member of the expedition team begins to allow others to carry his or her backpack, it can become a serious burden and compromise the entire expedition. Of course, there are situations when folks are going through tough times and need a helping hand, but when it becomes a chronic occurrence, you as the leader need to make a change. If you don't, you might find yourself carrying two or three backpacks.

Put on a Good Attitude

Attitude is a choice. You can either choose to be an encourager or a complainer. You can choose to be positive or negative, a problem solver or a cynic, but the choice is yours. Yes, I understand there are chemical imbalances and medical conditions that preclude certain individuals from having complete control over their attitudes. However, they represent the anomaly and not the norm.

Recall from Chapter 3 what we learned about the Leapfrog Accountability concept. If you think it might be difficult to have a corrective conversation with a chronic *whiner* or *complainer,* you could use one of the LesKar evaluation forms as a starting point. Either the 'Individual Performance Evaluation' or the 'Leadership Evaluation' might be good, whichever you discern as being the best approach for you.

A simple illustration of attitude might be helpful at this juncture. I've heard it said that one's state of mind, or attitude, can be compared to a rocket or space shuttle. In the tip of the aircraft, you have the Central Processing Unit; the CPU represents your *mind.* You have the wings/ailerons which control the direction of the aircraft; that would be your *will.* And then you have the fuel;

which is your *emotions*. In the cockpit, you have a *being* who is the captain or the pilot; that would be you. You are in control of the thoughts you think. You are responsible for controlling your will and you control your emotions: not your boss, not your co-worker, not your spouse or family or anyone else. That said, if you are in a leadership position, you need to model a good attitude. Attitude reflects leadership.

Think about it this way for a moment; the sheet of music on the piano has nothing to do with what keys are actually depressed, and the keys have nothing to do with the intensity that is applied. Nor do the strings have anything to do with how much tension is placed on them. No, this is all done by the piano player himself. So it is with your attitude.

Remember Mr. Snotty Pants in Chapter 3? His bad attitude was killing the morale at Beacon Enterprises. Don't let that happen inside your organization. You are the leader, the "relentless encourager." Lead by example, be strong and courageous, and make changes to your organizational team when the situation calls for it. The life of the organization depends on it!

Attitude

"The longer I live, the more I realize the impact of attitude on life. Attitude, to me, is more important than facts. It is more important than the past, than education, than money, than circumstances, than failure, than successes, than what other people think or say or do. It is more important than appearance, giftedness or skill. It will make or break a company... a church... a home. The remarkable thing is we have a choice everyday regarding the attitude we will embrace for that day. We cannot change our past... we cannot change the fact that people will act in a certain way. We cannot change the inevitable. The only thing we can do is play on the one string we have, and that is our attitude. I am convinced that life is 10% what happens to me and 90% of how I react to it. And so it is with you... we are in charge of our Attitudes."[17]

- Charles Swindoll

---

[17] Used by permission

CHAPTER SEVEN

Organizational Team Development

Organizational Team Model

"We are not machines; we are people, with our own fingerprints of personality and potential."

- *C. William Pollard*

Having no desire to "reinvent the wheel," I simply use Patrick Lencioni's model taken from his book *The Five Dysfunctions of a Team*[18]. This model serves as the lens through which we view working together as a team. It's profoundly simple and really does capture the essence of what is required if a team is going to work well together.

So let's go through the Organizational Team Model. Again, all the credit here goes to Patrick Lencioni for coming up with this: we're just building upon what he already discovered.

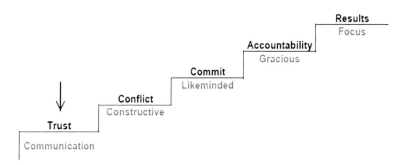

Trust

At the base of our Organizational Team Model is *Trust*. We say in our company that "the aggregate of trust is communication." This is not different than in your own family, your marriage or your relationship to a close friend. You trust them because you've had a lot of communication; you know them. Communication has allowed you to learn about them; what

---

[18] Patrick Lencioni, *The Five Dysfunctions of a Team,* (San Francisco: Josey-Bass, 2002)

they like or dislike, what their "hot buttons" are and what makes them "tick." The foundation for any relationship is trust, and it's not different in a team. If you can't trust the folks you're working with, you can't commit to the end result. And if there's not transparency, then there will never be trust. It's what Lencioni calls "vulnerability based trust"[19]: a trust where folks say things like "I don't know the answer to this...I made a mistake...I need help...I'm not good at this..." Or they say things like "I'm sorry about what I said yesterday, I was out of line."[20] As a leader of the team, you can set the example by starting to be vulnerable in those ways. As we mentioned earlier, you're going to have to start exercising humility. Pride often keeps us from being transparent or vulnerable.

Two other great resources on this subject are Stephen M.R. Covey's book *The Speed of Trust* and *The Revolutionary Communicator* by Jedd Medefind and Erik Lokkesmoe.

[19] Patrick Lencioni, *HSM Global, Think Beyond The Boardroom,* 2009 http://us.hsmglobal.com/contenidos/videoteca_detalle.html?idAdjunto=38615
[20] Ibid

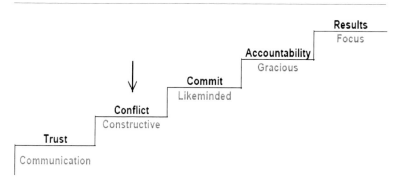

Conflict

If we enter into a relationship, team or personal, with open and honest communication and acknowledge there will, in fact, be conflict, I've discovered it exposes a white elephant. We have a rule about conflict – it can never be personal or condescending.

Embracing the fact that there will indeed be conflict is not different than embracing what is known in the Strength and Conditioning world as *The Overload Principle*. The Overload Principle states that as adaptation to an overload occurs, more of a load is required; and growth without resistance cannot occur. As a high school and college athlete, a Certified Strength and Conditioning Specialist and volunteer coach and trainer for over 20 years, I can tell you with confidence that this is true. Whether in a gym or on the road jogging for physical conditioning or in a classroom for learning or building a relationship, we must embrace and apply The Overload Principle. Know going in that *conflict* is the *resistance* that we will experience while growing together. But again, don't allow the conflict to get personal or condescending.

One more thing on conflict before we move on; in our company we have gotten comfortable enough with each other that we will say, "Okay, I think we're entering conflict." What this does is remove any presuppositions about anyone's "feelings" and lets everyone know that we may have a healthy wrestling match about to take place. We then have an opportunity to get everyone's thoughts out on the table for open and honest dialogue.

If we cannot trust that conflict between team members will remain healthy and constructive, then it will be impossible for us to *commit* to the team, the project, the company or whatever it is we are endeavoring to accomplish. This takes us to the next principle of the Organizational Team Development model, which is *Commit.*

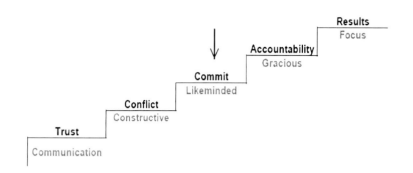

Commit

Are you committed? Is your team committed? Are they likeminded in an effort to achieve the same goal? If not, why? If you're honest, I'm sure you can think of a time in your own life when you were *not,* in fact, committed to the work you were doing. There are a number of reasons: perhaps you inherited a failed project, you were stuck with a team you didn't like in the first place, you didn't trust the leader, or perhaps you might have simply been in the wrong job. This is where you, as the leader, must find out from each of the team members whether they are or are not committed.

I would first recommend a one-on-one meeting with each of the team members to find out where they stand, and then follow it up in a team or staff meeting. Everyone needs to hear everyone else say they are committed to the project. This may sound corny, but when you get someone to actually commit to their peers, the bar is indeed raised. And I'll say it again, lead by example.

Accountability

The very word itself is kind of "prickly," is it not? If there were an object you could assign to the word "accountability," I think it might be a cactus. It's not at all like the word "relief" or "soothing." Those two words just seem to role off your tongue. Not "accountability." Six prickly syllables; sticking, poking, prodding and scratching at every dimension of your behavior. The word "hippopotamus" doesn't frighten us, and yet it represents a 6,000 lb. animal that eats baby elephants for dinner. Why do you suppose none of us like *accountability*?

In Chapter 3 we discussed accountability on an organizational level, using a very simple one page evaluation form, all in an effort to keep the organization informed and accountable. This is a little different; while it is still accountability, this is peer-to-peer accountability. This is up close and personal.

The way Lencioni sees it, if team members are not committed, they will avoid accountability. I don't disagree with his assessment but I might push that a little further. A person can be TOTALLY committed to a project and not want accountability, and this simply stems from pride. Let's be honest here; no one likes people "looking over their shoulder." Oh, come on! With your "inside voice," you've said on more than one occasion, "I don't need you looking over my shoulder," referring to your teacher, your boss or perhaps a family member or your spouse. And if you never have said or thought that, then you can move on to the next section of this book. For those of us who have said or thought that, let's take a moment to dissect this a little further.

The fact of the matter is, and I'll use myself as an example, I do need accountability. I do need speed limit signs, I do need stop signs, I do need my wife to frown or call me down when I get on a rant, I do need my friends to say, "Don't do that; it's not good for you." I did need my teacher to correct me when I made an error, I did need my dad to light me up when I got "too big for my britches," I do need there to be "No Trespassing" signs, I do need to obey the laws of the land, go to church and surround myself with a few close friends that will challenge me in how to be a better husband or dad. I do need to respect those in authority over me, and you know something else, I do need my employees to call me out for being late to a meeting, not following through with a task or acting inappropriately in a conversation or meeting.

Referring back to the Overload Principle, accountability is a way for us to grow. Here's a word picture for you: we need to look at accountability as the dolphins in our lives that keep the sharks of selfishness and pride from attacking our character.

Those that don't want or like accountability are the ones who say, "You can't tell me what to do," all the while telling us what not to do.

When holding one another accountable, we need to make sure we're doing it with grace, not "nit picking" at everyone for every minor infraction, but rather graciously encouraging our peers in accomplishing what we have set out to do. Using our expedition as an example, let's say "Joe" was falling behind: "Come on, Joe. Do you always have to be the last one up the hill? Y'know, maybe if you weren't such a loser, it wouldn't be so hard." Instead, you might say something like, "Keep it up, Joe. I know it's tough, but we're almost there. Can I give you a hand?"

Sounds elementary, but it will set a good example, and it may be all Joe needs to get to the top.

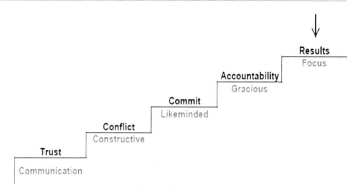

Results

The last principle on our Organizational Team Model is *results*. In his book *Good to Great*, Jim Collins identified what he coined the "Hedgehog Concept." Hedgehogs, said Collins, "...simplify a complex world into a single organizing idea, a basic principle or concept that unifies and guides everything."[21] Stated another way, hedgehogs were focused on results. Lencioni defined the last principle of his pyramid model this way: "Inattention to results occurs when team members put their individual needs (such as ego, career development, or recognition) or even the needs of their divisions above the collective goals of the team."[22]

If you stop and think about it, it's almost impossible to get good *results* in anything without *accountability*. And there can't be accountability without open *communication*. And open and honest communication stems from *trust*. Notice here we say trust and not "like." You don't have to like someone to trust them, but

---

[21] Jim Collins, *Good to Great,* (New York: HarperCollins, 2001), 91.
[22] Patrick Lencioni, *The Five Dysfunctions of a Team,* (San Francisco: Josey-Bass, 2002), 189.

you do have to communicate with them, and that communication does not always have to be verbal.

In our small company, we are required to provide monthly reports to our clients that fundamentally act as both an accountability and results mechanism. We include our deliverables in the Table of Contents of every report just so we're always focused on what we are doing, that is, *results*. It's important for the leader to constantly remind his colleagues why they are doing what they are doing. We call it "what done looks like." Jack Welch, in his book *Jack: Straight from the Gut,* said, "I was an outrageous champion of everything we did...whenever I had an idea or message I wanted to drive into the organization; I could never say it enough. I repeated it over and over and over, at every meeting and review, for years, until I could almost gag on the words."[23]

You cannot over-communicate your expectations for results.

In his best selling book, *The Soul of The Firm*, Bill Pollard wrote, "Our survival and future is dependent on [the team] working together in doing things right and in doing the right thing."[24]. In Organizational Team Development we don't see any of these principles as "either/or" but rather "both/and."

---

[23] Jack Welch w/ John A. Byrne, *Jack: Straight from the Gut* (New York: Business Plus, 2002), 393.
[24] C. William Pollard, *The Soul of The Firm,* (New York: HarperCollins, 1996), 29.

Part 3

Organizational Process Management

CHAPTER EIGHT

What Is Organizational Process Management?

or-gan-i-za-tion-al pro-cess man-age-ment

- description

the active effort of refining a series of rudimentary steps required to deliver a specified product or service.

I'm sure you've all heard about the old carpenter who quipped after throwing down his saw, "I cut that board three times and it's still too short." Too often we get so busy trying to stay ahead of the curve that we either don't take time to fix clunky processes, or perhaps we're just too lazy to fix them.

In the previous two sections we provided you with a few models through which you look at your organization and another through which you look at your teams or people. In this section we want to provide you a model through which you will look at your processes.

We've said that organizations are made up of people, processes and products. Processes, in a sense, are the glue that holds the people and the products together. Said another way, processes are the sheet of music people play from in delivering the products. If you've got good people playing off of good music, then chances are you'll have a good product.

Organizational Process Management is *a series of rudimentary steps required to deliver a specified product or service.* At various times in life or at work, there are moments, and sometimes even extended periods of time, when everyone seems to be heading in different directions. Without fail, someone will always sarcastically comment, "We're not all playing to the same sheet of music." What we all understand this to mean is that there is no order. Too often the person who is supposed to be in charge thinks he has given clear direction and can't understand how things have gone amuck.

In the next few chapters we will break down each of the *rudimentary steps* in Organizational Process Management that will provide you with a systematic approach in defining "what done looks like," all in an effort to create a symphony out of what may presently be a cacophony.

CHAPTER NINE

Is What You Are Doing Working?

Organizational Process Management Model

The definition of insanity is doing the same thing over and over again and expecting different results.

- Albert Einstein

I'll be honest with you, when my wife and I decided to build our first house, I thought – I presumed like every other "wanna be" carpenter in the world – that we could save some money if I just did some of the work myself. I mean, how hard can it be to hang some trim, install a few doors and hardware, build our closets, and so on? Well, to my surprise, it was not at all what I expected.

Like the carpenter I mentioned previously, every board I cut two and three times was still too short. Every door knob I put on always had the lock on the wrong side. Every door in our house works like it shouldn't. Most of the hardware on our cabinets is either not centered or isn't on at all – and, needless to say, not all of it is done yet. What I did wasn't working, and on many occasions, I would have to call in favors from friends who were actually qualified to come and help. I was always amazed at how easy they made it look, and it always turned out exactly the way it was supposed to. They understood their scope, and they understood the process.

I would like to ask you a few questions that I hope you will use in challenging each of your own internal processes:

Why are you doing what you're doing? Do the processes you have in place help you achieve the end product or do you do it just because "that's the way we've always done it"?

Is what you are doing working? I suppose that many of you reading this book would say, "For the most part, yes, but it could be better." Well how can we make it better?

Is what you are doing effective? "Not as effective as it could be" would be the predictable reply. Many processes can, indeed, be effective, but the residual fallout along the way is a disaster.

Is what you are doing efficient? Perhaps everyone is, in fact, busy-busy-busy, but what are they busy doing? What could your organization do, small or big, that would make it more efficient?

I can almost hear many readers saying (sarcastically), "...wow, those are some really profound questions! I've never heard those before (increased sarcasm). Glad I bought this book to learn those probing insights!" I would have said the same thing five years ago. But I would have added, "I *don't have time* to ask the questions, let alone answer them and implement whatever ideas we would come up with." And at the time, in the flurry I was in, you would have had a difficult time selling me on trying to improve the environment I was in. If that's you, read on!

Unlike the simple handy man tasks I was trying to accomplish when building my own home, I presume many of you have jobs or companies that require working with several other people or companies, with many different steps and processes necessary to deliver the end product and a lot of other factors that are peculiar to your business. So it is in my company, and after years and years of "grinding through to the end," we have developed what I believe to be a very helpful model that will, if used correctly, alleviate a lot of the frustration, improve expectations, help people understand who needs to do what, and at the same time provide clarity to those around you. Might I also add that it stimulates teamwork, invites accountability and cultivates transparency? We call it Organizational Process Management.

As you learned earlier, Organizational Process Management is *a series of rudimentary steps required to deliver a specified product or service.* It acts, as we stated earlier, as the glue that holds our people and our product together; or the sheet of music that we all play to when striving to accomplish what it is we set out to do.

I am well aware that our model will not solve all of your processional woes and does not replace complicated process algorithms. It is not intended to replace what you are currently doing. It is simply meant to provide clarity to what you already know needs to be done. After all, the sheet of music does not replace the instrument, but rather acts as a roadmap for the musician. My hope is that you will use this model as a kind of "joystick" for steering the organization. I believe it will aide in instruction, reinforce documentation, facilitate organization and invite accountability. I know it will help you in challenging the process, which is what effective leaders do when striving for improvement.

CHAPTER TEN

Implementing Organizational Process Management

Organizational Process Management Model

One thing is sure. We have to do something. We have to do the
best we know how at the moment... if it doesn't turn out right, we
can modify it as we go along.

-    *Franklin D. Roosevelt*

What organization wouldn't want better processes? Changing processes is a lot of work, but what we are suggesting is not a complete "overhaul" of what you are currently doing. Chances are, if what you were doing was completely wrong, you wouldn't be where you are today.

Several years ago I joined Ernst & Young, who later merged with Cap Gemini, and since I had a host of experiences with previous employers in implementing Standard Operating Procedures, I was hired to provide what is known as Business Process Reengineering or (BPR). When we would arrive at a client facility, we were charged with evaluating every aspect of their processes and sort out the good from the bad, the inefficient from the efficient, then streamline their processes to help them more efficiently achieve what they were trying to accomplish. I cannot recall even one time where we totally ditched what they were doing. We did, however, always find unnecessary steps that were being taken that most often were a frustration to the entire team.

Based upon my experience with those clients, I presume what you are doing could use a little tune up, using a simple model to evaluate your Standard Operating Procedures – or overall processes.

As you have seen at the start of each chapter in this section, we have what we call our Organizational Process Management Model. As we have done in the previous chapters, let us look closely at each of the steps.

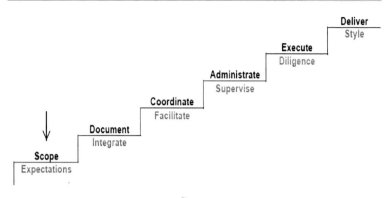

Scope

The first order of business on the Organizational Process Model is *Scope,* getting everyone to understand what it is you are doing. Our goal is to uncover all of the expectations and assumptions that go with the assignment, project, deliverable or whatever. Sounds easy enough, but exactly how far do you push this? My experience, especially during the implementation phase, is that you, the leader, must always assume that it is each team member's first day on the job; certainly, explain the overall scope of the project. If your team is qualified in their unique roles, you may assume they have a general grasp of what it is you are doing. For example, I assume that if you are in the software or technology industry, you don't have a journeyman mason on the team. I would say you probably have qualified software or electrical engineers or information technology folks who understand programming and the various languages and nuances of the software programming industry, not someone who shows up with a trowel and a four foot level. That person would certainly be on the wrong team.

What I'm talking about is facilitating input of the obvious. Let's say you have a new project coming up, and for the most part it isn't any different than any other project you've done in the past except that it has the usual idiosyncrasies that appear on every new project. As in the past, everyone has similar roles and responsibilities as they've always had, except this time we are going to hold a brief Organizational Process Management (OPM) meeting where we're going to go through each of the steps necessary for the new project. Then, on a weekly basis we are going to "reinforce" what we talked about (i.e. over-communicate).

In the *Scope* phase, the goal is to get *everything* out on the table; starting off with "What is the end product?" and, in your mind, "What does done look like?" That is the obvious, and you probably already do that anyway. You then want to make certain you get your *expectations and assumptions* out on the table:

- What the overall goals of the project are
- What the objectives are (i.e. effort needed to achieve each goal)
- What the idiosyncrasies of this project are
- What time you expect everyone to start
- How much time each day you expect them to spend on the project
- What attitude you expect them to bring to the project. This was discussed in Chapter 6 and this is where you as the leader need to reinforce attitude issues.

- The kind of reporting you expect
- The frequency of reporting
- What you expect the report to look like (i.e. the format)
- Role identification and responsibilities
- What "players" are needed to complete this project (subs, consultants, staff, et al)
- What your expectations are for each of the subcontractors, consultants or other team members
- What milestones you hope to hit by what date
- The project deadline
- What the desired outcome is. This is a big one and SHOULD NOT be ignored. What exactly do you desire the outcome to be at each milestone, as well as at the end?

The list can go on, but you get where I'm going with this. GET EVERYTHING OUT ON THE TABLE!

All too often false expectations and assumptions are what kill a project. "Well, you never said that…I didn't know that's what you meant…we've never done that in the past…why didn't you tell me in the first place…I thought so and so was doing that…since when was I in charge of that?", and on and *ad nauseum* it goes.

What we're talking about here is "getting everyone on the same page" from the onset. It appears on the surface that this is really elementary, and it is. The book titled *Everything I Need to Know I Learned in Kindergarten* became a New York Times bestseller and sold over seven million copies. That book was not about Organizational Process Management, but I believe we can use it as an example of the desirability of simply getting back to the basics. Work doesn't need to be that complicated, and typically, it's not the complicated things that keep a project from being a success. Trouble comes from straying away from the fundamentals. I've often said it's not the rock in the road that keeps the walker from finishing, but rather the small stone in the bottom of his shoe. The same can be said for successfully completing a project; it's the little things that create the biggest frustration.

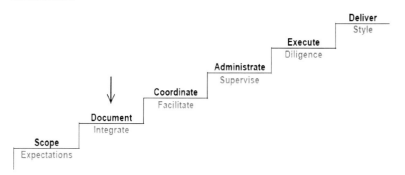

Document

This, too, sounds simple enough, but we've all been there; sitting across from the angry peer, client, consultant, owner, subcontractor, child, wife, whoever. So you talked about some element in the beginning, but did you write it down? Understand that if we're talking about holding a small kick-off meeting with the team, the level of documentation will look dramatically different than if you're signing up a third party subcontractor or consultant to a multi-million dollar contract. But the same principles apply in either case; write it down! Yes, even those elementary assumptions.

If you are in a small kick-off meeting, then I would recommend that you have someone take notes, and after the meeting, distribute what was discussed. In our company, we call them Work Plans. These will be discussed more extensively in Chapter 15 of this book. They may be a lengthy document, or they can be as simple as a single sheet of copy paper with hand written notes. You'll have to determine what best fits the occasion.

The point is writing everything down; all of the expectations, all of the assumptions, everything. Then circulate it, have everyone sign it, and don't lose it, because you'll want to refer to it often. When I say often, I mean in staff meetings, over e-mail, in the hall, in the bathroom, in a monthly memo – over-communicate it.

I want to remind those in leadership positions to do this in an encouraging way, not in a nagging, whining, guilt-ridden way, but rather in a positive, friendly, up-beat, "can do" way. Remember you are to be the "relentless encourager."

Integration goes hand-in-hand with good documentation. What you have documented must be integrated into the actual project. I know in my business, one of the biggest issues we run into is forgetting what was documented. In my profession, for whatever reason, once a contract is signed, whether for thousands or millions or tens of millions of dollars, it is then stowed away in a beautiful classification folder with it's own label and placed in a hermetically sealed envelope and seldom looked at ever again, that is, until all chaos has broken loose and your into the yelling, screaming, spitting and finger pointing phase. Why? Because what was discussed during the OPM meeting, fleshed out in the expectations and assumptions session and then documented, has not been integrated into a routine scheduled scope review. Who has time for that? I mean, really, it's so much easier just talking in generalities and assuming everyone understands and remembers what was discussed three or four months ago, right? Wrong.

In Chapter 7, I mentioned that we are required to provide our clients a monthly report. In the beginning of that report we actually have our scope listed. Once a month we meet with our clients to go through that report and discuss each one of those scope items in detail. This meeting takes no more than 45 minutes to an hour and keeps everyone on the same page. And can I be totally honest with you? Not a month goes by that I don't find myself nodding my head and saying (with my inside voice), "Oh, yeah. We need to follow up on that."

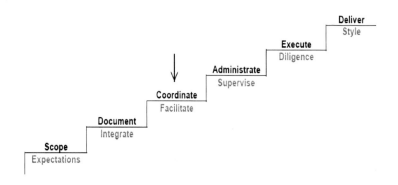

Coordinate

Who doesn't understand *coordinate*? I mean how hard can that be? You call, e-mail or meet with the relevant parties, share the overall intent and some generalities about the scope, sign'em up and you are off to the races. Then you're done right? Well, in a perfect world, maybe; in this world, no.

In the next few pages we're going to flesh out *coordinate, administrate* and *execute.* They are terms that certainly share similarities, but are, in fact, different. If not addressed separately, you will leave gaps that turn into large cracks that lead to structural failure and result in total collapse.

Different businesses sometimes assign different titles to these tasks, but nonetheless, all of these functions need to be done.

If I were to bet, my guess would be that everyone reading this book has had a time in their life where they have either heard or experienced something to the effect, "Oh, I thought my assistant (coordinator) was doing that," or, "I gave all of that information to them (administrator); I don't understand why that didn't get done" or, "I told those guys exactly what to do, and it still didn't get done (execution)."

In those situations what we're saying is no one gave – or not everyone received – clear direction, a cogent plan or the necessary means to complete what was assigned. In other words, they didn't have an Organizational Process Model that provided the necessary checks and balances to assure a successful project delivery. Or perhaps they did and it still didn't get done. There are a lot of great companies out there that have this dialed but still struggle with execution. Why? Read on and perhaps you'll find out.

To *coordinate* means to bring something into common action, movement or to act together in a certain way; to harmonize. Who on your team is acting in the capacity to make that happen? Are they truly bringing all of the parts and pieces or people together? Is all of the necessary information efficiently transmitted and copied to the pertinent players? Are all of the right people attending the meetings that determine what needs to happen?

I remember giving a presentation to a prospective client. I was making my way up the Organizational Process Management Model, he interrupted me and said, "Yeah, yeah, all that stuff." He went on to tell me, "We have a model that we use; we call it

K.I.S.S.; Keep it Simple, Stupid." I smiled and kindly replied, "Exactly! That's why we use the OPM Model."

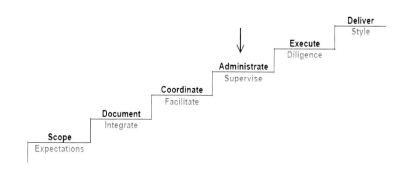

Administrate

The definition of *administrate* is to manage or supervise the affairs of execution. Managing or supervising the affairs of execution, is not executing. How many of you have said yourself, or heard someone say, "It's just easier if I do it myself." That may be true, but if you're managing or supervising several projects, or small projects within a big project, or managing or supervising several people, the organization as a whole will suffer. The folks who are suppose to be doing the *executing* won't be allowed the opportunity to succeed, will be enabled to fail, and you, as the *administrator,* will lose focus of the big picture.

Let me illustrate with a bit of family life. We've all been there either as a child or a parent. Mom or dad asks a child to clean his room, and he doesn't. Mom or dad gets mad and does it for him. This becomes the practice and the   child does not learn the virtue of cleanliness or organization.   In addition, mom or dad is now burdened with yet another responsibility – which is the child's responsibility – and the entire family suffers. And the old saying is confirmed, "When mamma ain't happy, ain't nobody happy."

Remember in Chapter 6 we learned that everyone is supposed to pull his own weight, otherwise the entire expedition to the summit is compromised. When quarterbacks are forced to scramble, the turn-over rate increases, not to mention their vulnerability to injury. When *administrators* are forced to scramble, the efficiency of the entire organization, as well as the success of the project, is compromised.

As an administrator, you must learn the art of delegation. "Whether delegating vertically or horizontally, delegation must be accompanied by effective coaching. Delegation will not be effective unless managers and other designated supervisors and coaches work with employees to help them develop the skills needed to get the job done. Effective delegation also requires good communication and a high degree of trust between the delegator and the delegatee."[25] The art of delegation brings in two important principles that were previously discussed in Chapters 4 and 7; *trust*, which is the foundation of the Organizational Team Development Model, and the seventh principle of the LesKar Principles of Sustainability – *train to go.*

---

[25] Directory Journal, "How to Effectively Delegate," http://www.dirjournal.com/guides/how-to-delegate-effectively/

Something else worth emphasizing here is that delegating is not limited vertically, but should be encouraged and practiced horizontally. Quoting again from "How to Effectively Delegate," *"The inability to delegate has led to the downfall of many executives* – from the top-notch managers to the first-line supervisors. Successful businesses, regardless of size, encourage not only their managers and supervisors but also others to master the art of delegation. Historically, delegation has been a vertical process, with managers delegating to subordinates in a clearly defined hierarchical structure. Today's successful businesses are emphasizing both horizontal and vertical delegation. With the growing emphasis on teamwork, the ability to influence and delegate to others over whom you have no direct control is critical to the team's success."[26]

Is your organization providing the necessary support needed to effectively *administrate?* How does your team or organization as a whole do in delegating? How could it be better? Do you as the *administrator* or *supervisor* take time to explain and teach what needs to be done – or at a minimum express your *expectations and assumptions* to provide a clear explanation to subordinates or other team members of "what done looks like"?

---

[26] Ibid

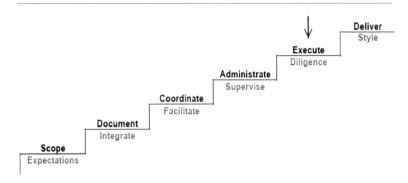

Execute

If *administrating* means to manage or supervise the affairs of execution, *to execute* means to carry out fully; put completely into effect; produce or perform what is required. It should now be very clear to the reader that *administrating* is not *executing.*

Effective execution requires clear direction, cogent planning and the means to accomplish what is required. I was recently having a discussion with a good friend of mine who was a Senior Program Manager in the Engineering & Product Development department for an aviation company that built private jets. The company started with an extraordinarily advanced design using the latest technology and had spent years perfecting the entire process to produce this one-of-a-kind aircraft. From engineering, to planning, to processing, to assembly, the company was being touted as one of the most advanced aerospace companies ever, in their respective field.

They had the people, they *thought* they had the process, they had the state of the art product – and they had the money. From the time they took the first order for their first aircraft until the day they closed the doors was less than ten years. The problem? Execution! The production of a plane that was suppose to take only 72 hours from start to finish was taking two to three weeks. It wasn't that they weren't getting orders – they had more than enough deposits for new planes. It wasn't that the aircraft couldn't fly or was experiencing problems – they won one of the most prestigious awards in the aeronautical industry. No, the problem was simple execution.

Installation defects required a plane to be pulled from the assembly line, sometimes for days, sometimes for weeks; all to fix or re-engineer the plane to be put back into production. The folks in the assembly line had received thorough training. However, sometimes the skill set of the individual did not match the job. Sometimes problems were caused by a poor attitude of the assembly line person. Sometimes the sheer repetition and redundancy led to complacency. Either problem led to improper execution and ultimately the demise of the company.

I ask you again; is what you are doing working? Is one small process precluding you from executing what needs to happen? Or perhaps it's several small processes. Whatever the case, I would like to challenge you to challenge your processes to execute.

If you are the *administrator/supervisor,* I would like to encourage you to lead the challenge. It could save your organization.

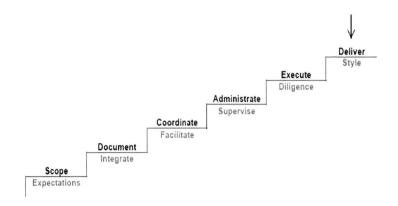

Deliver

This is the last step in the Organizational Process Management model, but it may be the most important. Many a flailing company has survived inefficiencies in fleshing out a clear *scope.* To be honest, a lot of companies really aren't that good at *documentation.* The demise of just about every organization is poor *coordination.* Yet we all have either worked with, or know personally, individuals who have been promoted to *Administrators* (substitute Superintendent, C.E.O., Executive, V.P. or whatever) in a poorly coordinated organization, and somehow they are still able to keep their job and the organization afloat.

How? By *delivering* in style.

I have either worked for or consulted for companies who were both good and bad at this. The ones who are good at *delivering* in style are the ones who take a genuine interest in their clients as individuals, who know them personally, overlook their selfish overreaching demands, who answer their calls on weekends, who go out of their way to please the client, who practice "the client's always right" attitude, who will – without putting the entire organization at risk – go the extra mile to keep the relationship. In spite of all of their own shortcomings and company flaws, they retain their clients and get the referral in the end. Fundamentally, at the end of the day, in humility, they consider others more important than themselves.

And, I have also worked for or consulted to organizations which were awful at *delivering* in style.

They do not care about their clients. It's all about the bottom line at the end of the day. They look for ways to get out of an obligation rather than do something as a gracious gesture to cultivate a trustworthy relationship. At the end of the day, they are in it for themselves and go about their work with an attitude of "I was looking for a job when I found this one" rather than with a "can do" attitude. They do not value a relationship as a potential future client."

A good example of *delivering* in style is when I go into the place where I buy my tires and they remember who I am. And if they don't, they act like they're glad to see me. When they take my truck to rotate the tires, they get me a cup of coffee while I wait, greet me with a smile when they are done and sincerely thank me for my business when I leave. Later, they call me to see if everything is okay and ask if everything is working like it should. *Delivering* in style is the realtor who sends a housewarming gift when you move in, sends Christmas cards every year and occasionally calls to see how you're doing. Delivering in style is getting a hand written note from the *Administrator* or C.E.O. saying thank you and that he hopes we can work together again.

In his book *Swim with the Sharks Without Being Eaten Alive,* Harvey Mackay provides an exhaustive list of what he coins the "66 Question Customer Profile,"[27] an exhaustive survey used to understand and know the customer. Later in the book, he provides a short lesson called "Short Notes Yield Long Results."[28] In summary, he says to take the time to write a short note of encouragement to everyone around you – especially your customer.

I have a few questions for you: What is the most common problem with your organization's processes in successfully delivering a project? What is the solution? Are you challenging the processes? Are you going out of your way to over-deliver to your client? Are you asking the entire team these questions? Or are you,

---

[27] Harvey Mackay, *Swim with the Sharks Without Being Eaten Alive*, (New York: William Morrow and Company; 1988), p. 46
[28] Ibid, p.68

in the words of Albert Einstein, "doing the same things over and over and expecting different results"?

Part 4

Organizational Product Mapping

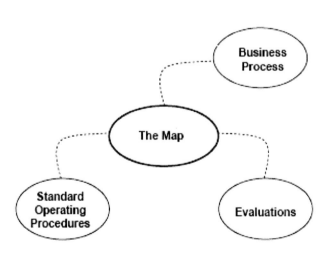

CHAPTER ELEVEN

Directional Dyslexia?

or-gan-i-za-tion-al pro-duct map-ping

- description

2. *a graphical representation of the various phases and stages of a project*

I have a confession to make: yours truly suffers with what I have coined *Directional Dyslexia*. I don't believe I'm alone, and quite honestly, I think most men suffer from this deplorable disease. I do also believe I have discovered the root cause – PRIDE!

We've all been there, folks – you know the feeling. You're driving with your wife and kids (or other comrades) in an unfamiliar area. You've been given directions by someone, and you are certain you know where you're going, so certain that any audible frequencies muttered are totally blocked out by your intense concentration. You turn right (when you should have turned left). You proceed slowly for about 2 miles and then get an uncontrollable urge to accelerate. Exceeding the speed limit by at least a factor of two, you then, with violent and aggressive precision, abruptly press on the brake to make an immediate left and quickly return to the speed you were driving before braking and turning. You sense internally that you may, in fact, be lost but don't dare let anyone in the car know. After all, you are the captain of this ship and the captain must always remain calm. You proceed for another couple of miles before those audible mutterings that you were previously able to block out suddenly penetrate with a piercing impact. Still not willing to concede, you proceed with an even greater fervor. You begin to slow, looking this way and that, just hoping – beyond all hope – that the address that has eluded you will suddenly appear. After a few jolting brake slams and a few quick "pump fake" turns from what you thought was the road sign you were looking for, you finally concede the unthinkable and dejectedly make the most dreaded confession of your life: "We're lost." Quick to recover just a semblance of dignity, you reassure your traveling companions, with "Well, we're not TOTALLY lost…at least we're in the right city."

Having completely lost the joyful expectant ambience you started out with on your little journey, and now trying to console your closest of kin, you pull into a service station and get what you should have had from the beginning – a map.

Doesn't it also ring somewhat true with a project or a business? Everything seems so exciting at the start, doesn't it? And about a quarter of the way through, you notice things aren't going as expected. Attitudes begin to change, the people start to grumble, you start to lose focus and begin to concentrate on all of the negatives. Deadlines start to slip, the goals start to fade and it's almost as if a fog begins to settle over the entire project that obscures everyone's vision.

This, however, is precisely the time when the leader must step forward, survey his "organizational dashboard," determine what vitals are not functioning properly, take out his compass and provide the direction that everyone needs in order to reach the ultimate destination. Sounds a bit cliché, but it's true.

And that is what this section is all about; giving you a literal roadmap that removes the obscurity hindering achievement and provides the entire team a clear picture of what needs to be done.

CHAPTER TWELVE

Would You Like Me to Draw You a Map?

"In the presence of great art and beauty we inescapably feel that there is real meaning in life…"

- Timothy Keller

At the start of Part 4 we defined Organizational Product Mapping as *a graphic illustration that provides a visual image or picture of the various phases and stages of a project;* not unlike the usual roadmap you have seen and used a thousand times before. We will now take you through what we believe will become the way organizations in the future not only share their business model and vision, but display it graphically.

Organizational Product Mapping acts as a 3-dimensional model wherein the process of getting from A to Z is graphically shown. Evaluations are embedded and easily accessible and the Standard Operating Procedures of the organization are made available to the entire team. When complete, there is never any confusion on how and when things need to be done. Predictably, you are now asking, "So how is Organizational Product Mapping different than our typical organizational planning?"

Organizational Product Mapping is different from traditional organizational planning in that it provides a visual aide – or again a "roadmap" – that captures the essence of one's vision by graphically representing, in a three-dimensional illustration, important concepts that a team leader desires to communicate. It also allows a more inviting medium for members of the organization to participate, own, and see how each of their respective roles play into the overall plan. Different also from the traditional thesis, report or business plan that simply communicates in a one-dimensional way, Organizational Product

Mapping gives the audience and team a single "take-away" that can be displayed and referred to on a daily basis.

I am not suggesting that organizations have not been successful or cannot succeed without Organizational Product Mapping, as there are countless thousands of businesses and organizations over the past century that have operated and functioned without ever having even heard of this. But businesses, by the introduction of new means and technology, can improve and become more effective under their current operating model.

The vivid imagery of a graphic 3-dimensional image of the overall project or plan challenges everyone on the team to think about their respective roles:

What happens before and after their task in process?

How does this affect the ultimate outcome?

How does this affect the team?

What could be done to improve the process?

How can I create a model for my own department/team/division?

Here's the point: over the past several decades the computer industry has made amazing progress in providing their end user with a much easier and more graphical user interface. Yet in the same period of time at the Organizational Management level we have continued using the same old management tools we've always used. I'm not saying they are not effective, but I am saying they could be improved.

Using Organizational Product Mapping, leaders can now challenge their team members to create interactive maps as they, too, are on a "Project Expedition" of their own. When this is done throughout an organization, you then have an entire team that understands what the end game is, what the processes are, and just how critical it is for each individual to do his part. Additionally, an Organizational Product Map provides a portal through which Standard Operating Procedures can be accessed. Organizational Product Maps assure that all of the most up-to-date documents are being used and that each step of the process is being followed.

Consider a few of the examples below that represent the visual shift in technology we are talking about:

DOS	**To**	Windows
Pager	**To**	Smart-phone
2 Dimensional drawing	**To**	3-Dimensional rotating
Verbal Directions	**To**	Written Directions
Written Directions	**To**	Map
Map	**To**	GPS

We are not suggesting that any of the items listed on the left are obsolete; quite the contrary. What we are doing is simply presenting how different the two types of communication are and how one can be more effective in presentation than the other.

Consider for a moment the traditional Process Flow Charts (algorithms) that are commonly used to capture the logic used in a simple process:

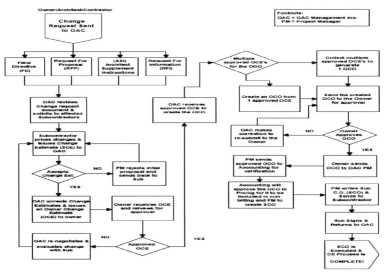

Let's take a look at a traditional sequence of events for a typical project as communicated on a common Gantt Chart.

Activity ID	Activity Description	Orig Dur	Total Float	Early Start	Early Finish	2007	2008	2009	2010
05-SUB-001	Submit on Stairs	75		25MAR08A	21APR08A	Submit on Stairs			
09-SUB-005	Submit on floorcoverings	55	49	26MAR08A	03FEB09		Submit on floorcoverings		
16-SUB-014	Submit on Lightning Protection	25		04APR08A	12AUG08A		Submit on Lightning Protection		
16-SUB-017	Subcontractor prepare Pre-Fab Dwg RFI #386.R1	40		16APR08A	17JUN08A		Subcontractor prepare Pre-Fab Dwg RFI #386.R1		
08-SUB-002	Submit on wood doors & hardware	45		29APR08A	22AUG08A		Submit on wood doors & hardware		
02-SUB-001	Submit on granular backfill materials	25		21MAY08A	24JUN08A		Submit on granular backfill materials		
09-SUB-003	Submit on Drywall Systems	100		21MAY08A	30OCT08A		Submit on Drywall Systems		
16-SUB-008	Submit on Tele/Data	25		22MAY08A	27AUG08A		Submit on Tele/Data		
16-SUB-011	Submit on Intrusion Detection	25	74	09JUN08A	06FEB09		Submit on Intrusion Detection		
05-SUB-002	Submit on Steel Structure (Center and West)	25	59	16JUN08A	27FEB09		Submit on Steel Structure (Center and West)		
15-SUB-320	Submit fire sprinkler system	100		25JUN08A	26JAN09A		Submit fire sprinkler system		
12-SUB-001	Submit on pool & saunas	45	71	27JUN08A	23FEB09		Submit on pool & saunas		
10-SUB-005	Submit fireplaces	45		30JUN08A	28OCT08A		Submit fireplaces		
10-SUB-003	Submit on Signage	60	71	01JUL08A	27MAR09		Submit on Signage		
16-SUB-003	Submit on Lighting Control	25		04AUG08A	12AUG08A		Submit on Lighting Control		
16-SUB-006	Submit on Primary Electrical Switchgear & Eq	15		04AUG08A	22AUG08A		Submit on Primary Electrical Switchgear & Eq		
16-SUB-009	Submit on Bi-Directional Antenna	25		04AUG08A	29AUG08A		Submit on Bi-Directional Antenna		
16-SUB-013	Submit on Security	25	33	04AUG08A	06FEB09		Submit on Security		
16-SUB-010	Submit on Sound System	25		06AUG08A	12AUG08A		Submit on Sound System		
08-SUB-013	Submit on Access Control	25	19	13AUG08A	16FEB09		Submit on Access Control		
10-SUB-001	Submit on bathroom accessories	45	47	15AUG08A	17FEB09		Submit on bathroom accessories		

Neither of these ways needs to be replaced because it is wrong. But there is now a better way to communicate the overall essence of a project that captures each phase, milestone, key events, reporting and other important activities. Consider for a moment the effect this would have in sales presentations to prospective clients. Unlike the other mediums, an entire team is able to see the "Big Picture" and even access the necessary documents needed to accomplish each phase, milestone or task – right from their own computer.

An Organization Product Map might look something like this:

Most people don't think in algorithms or Gantt Charts. We are image and object driven creatures. It's what the world around us gives to the eye. If you are making a long trip across the state or country, you don't typically sit down and draw out an algorithm or create a Gantt Chart. No, you go for a map. When you look online for directions, you don't get a complete legal description; you get a map with additional written, step-by-step instructions.

Different? Indeed. Useful? Very. Effective? Incredibly. Efficient? Yes. So why am I not doing this? Good question. In the next chapter we'll tell you how.

"If a man has once looked at the Atlantic from the beach, and then goes and looks at a map of the Atlantic, he also will be turning from something real to something less real: tuning from real waves to a bit of colored paper. But here comes the point. The map is admittedly only colored paper, but there are two things you have to remember about it. In the first place, it is based on what hundreds and thousands of people have found out by sailing the real Atlantic. In that way it has behind it masses of experience just as real as the one you could have from the beach; only, while yours would be a single isolated glimpse, the map fits all those different experiences together. In the second place, if you want to go anywhere, the map is absolutely necessary. As long as you are content with walks on the beach, your own glimpses are far more fun than looking at a map. But the map is going to be more use than walks on the beach if you want to get to America."[29]

- C.S. Lewis

---

[29] C.S. Lewis, *Mere Christianity* (New York: Macmillan, 1952), 135.

CHAPTER THIRTEEN

How Do You Make One?

"In the presence of great art and beauty we inescapably feel that there is real meaning in life..."

- Timothy Keller

You may remember in the movie *The Greatest Game Ever Played* when Francis Ouimet's caddy, Eddie Lowery, calms him before a difficult putt with the memorable words, "Easy peasy lemon squeazy." And so it is in creating an Organizational Product Map.

I think the easiest way to think about creating an Organizational Product Map is to think in terms of a graphical outline. I do not know what product your organization produces, but it could be anything from a widget to a car, a computer program, a service, a building, a bridge, a marketing campaign, a student, a child, a plate of food, a reformed person, or even a college education. Products and the organizations that make them are numerous. But the common thread that runs through them all is that they become what they become through a process. As I have stated throughout this book, none of what I am writing is new; it's just perhaps a different way of looking at what has been done, and in the writer's opinion, perhaps a better way of getting it done.

Step 1 - What Done Looks Like

The first order of business is to understand "what done looks like" (i.e. what is the end product). Before identifying the phases of the project, the leader must know and be able to articulate where he or she is taking the team. What is the end game? Project leaders must have in their mind's eye a convincingly strong grasp on what it is they are trying to achieve in the end; not that you must understand all of the minute details that are required to get you to the end, but rather a clear vision of what it is you are trying to accomplish.

We talked extensively in Part 3 of the book about fleshing out the *scope* and making sure all of the *expectations and assumptions* are understood. This will happen later on when you add detail to the map, but for now we're talking about making sure the map includes the desired destination.

A good exercise at this point is to simply grab a piece of paper, write the name of the project at the top and quickly make an outline of the project, starting by numbering the major component parts that make up the project.

Step 2 – Phasing

The second step in creating an Organizational Product Map is to identify what I call *phases*. Simply stated, these are the Roman numerals in your outline of what leads to the end product. In other words, what are the major component parts or aspects in creating your product?

Step 3 – Staging

Stages are the subcategories of your phases. Using an outline as an example, what are the capital letters under your Roman numerals in your outline? Within each phase you have another subset of component parts that are required to complete that phase. I would caution the leader not to drill down too far in identifying activities or certain tasks, but rather, in this step try to identify the big "chunks" of each phase.

Step 4 – Activities

After you have established your stages, you will want to begin to drill down and begin to evaluate what major activities will be necessary to achieve each milestone along with the path to the finished product. I want to again caution the person creating the map NOT to get too detailed in creating activities. If you have a series of related activities, you can easily lump these together and give them all a common name. I would recommend only 2 to 3 activities between each milestone. If you feel it is absolutely necessary to show an activity then do so; just be cognizant that too many activities on an Organizational Product Map can get confusing. What we have done in the past when we have several activities or steps that are needed to complete a certain phase or milestone is lump them together and then link those to another document that lists them in detail.

Step 5 – Milestones

The next step is to identify some major milestones that you will want to accomplish by a certain date. Milestones simply define the completion of a series of activities and are critical in that they give the project team a few intermittent goals to strive for. They punctuate when certain things need to get done in your effort to achieve the end goal. Milestones also allow for a time to celebrate, a time to commend and applaud the effort that has been put forth in achieving a portion of the overall project. Milestones allow the leader to reenergize the group with enthusiasm. I like what Chuck Swindoll said about enthusiasm: "Athletes feed on it. Salesmen are motivated by it. Teachers count on it. Students fail without it. Leadership demands it. Projects are completed because of it."[30] And as Ralph Waldo Emerson said, "Nothing great was ever achieved without enthusiasm."[31]

Milestones are also a great time to do performance evaluations for the organization as a whole, the team, the processes being used, as well as for individual evaluations.

Step 6 – Reporting

Upon completing your map with all of the phases, stages, activities, and milestones you will now want to add reporting symbols at certain places along the road where you believe you will want a Progress Update or Executive Summary, as we call them. These are represented using the little transmitter symbol shown on the sample map at the end of this section. By adding this symbol, your team will be visually reminded of when they have certain reports due. It's another way of graphically showing that there is *accountability* along the way. Since everyone's reports are different according to what types of information are needed or expected, we won't go into detail about that in this book. You can go to our website and see a sample of what might go into a report.

---

[30] Chuck Swindoll, Man to Man (Michigan: Zondervan, 1996), p.178.
[31] www.saidwhat.co.uk/quotes/famous/ralph_waldo_emerson

Step 7 – Evaluations

Once your map is populated with all of the essential symbols that will successfully lead you on your expedition, it is time to add the final icon that represents *evaluations.* These are denoted with a magnifying glass. Our recommendation is that at least one magnifying glass be placed in every phase of the expedition.

As was stated in Part 1, Chapter 1 of the book, our recommendation is that you evaluate your organization a minimum of one time per month. Whether you are evaluating the organization as a whole, the team, the processes, the individual, the leadership, or all of them, it is imperative to get feedback from the team on a frequent basis. This will only help you in creating a healthy culture of transparency, accountability and change. As the leader of your expedition, recognize that it is vital to the success of your overall team and organization that they have a voice, and that their concerns, recommendations or encouragements are heard. For a complete list of the LesKar evaluation forms to aid you in this step you can go to our website.

Step 8 – Project Essentials

This is the final step in creating your Organizational Product Map. Every organization has what we call their *project essentials.* These are simply all of the documents that are used in route to the expedition summit. Your project essentials would also include any and all templates that you are currently using or have used in the past. This part of creating your map could be the most laborious, but it is also the most critical.

Collecting your *project essentials* will also enable the team leader to assess all of the old templates and documents that so often rear their ugly head in the midst of a project. This is a great time to discard old forms, letters, checklists, contracts, reports or any other outdated documents, and "standardize."

I remember the first time we went through the process of collecting all of our *project essentials.* When we were through, it was as if I had just finished cleaning out my garage. (I've actually never done that, but I can now imagine what it would feel like if I did!) All of our logos were the same, things were added that we had intended to add several projects ago, processes were thought through and the entire team now knew what needed to be done.

Once you have all of your *project essentials* rounded up, you can place them in the "Base Camp" where they are easily accessed and referred to throughout the expedition. To some of you, this may sound a bit burdensome, and you may think I'm taking this whole map thing too far, but I would ask you to consider the following scenario:

Imagine you and a few other friends were actually going on an expedition or backpacking trip that would take you a week. Everyone arrives at the starting point (i.e. Base Camp) at the designated time, and off you go. You travel the first 8 to 10 miles and decide to camp for the first night. You all scout out your own little tent sites and get your tent set up just the way you like, and you all begin to gather around the fire pit. A few stomachs begin to growl, so you decide it's time to cook your first meal. Before leaving, you had all decided who would bring what and how everyone would contribute to the meal time gala. As each person begins to perform their respective duties, one of the team members cries out, "Okay, who brought the cooking utensils?" Nervously, everyone looks around and discovers no one actually brought any cooking utensils. After a few snide comments from ole Mr. Snotty Pants (yes he's still around), the blame game begins. Everyone finally shrugs it off and decides to roast their chicken breasts over the fire using some make-shift skewers from a nearby shrub. The next morning everyone is happy that Tom brought a soda, as his empty soda can is used as the only frying pan to cook the scrambled eggs – and off you go on day two.

Up the trail you go, and it begins to narrow and disappear, and you reach not only a fork but a prong in your path. Not familiar with where you are, everyone's head cranes around looking for the "guide" to ask him which trail you need to take. Quickly, the guide begins to rifle through his backpack only to discover that he not only forgot his map, but he also forgot his compass. Risky bunch that you are, someone makes a confident wave of his arm, and the team heads off in an unknown direction. And you can see where the story is going from here.

The point is this; we would no more head out on a five day backpacking trip without checking, double checking and triple checking that everyone had their "essentials" than we would try to tame a 40 ton squid. But all too often, and I'm guilty myself, we will start a multi-million dollar project and not take the time to check and double check the "project essentials" to make certain they are not only in perfect functioning order, but that everyone understands and clearly knows who is doing what along the way.

Let's review the eight steps necessary to create an Organizational Product Map:

Step 1 – Understand "*What done looks like*"

Step 2 – Determine the *Phases*

Step 3 – Identify the *Stages*

Step 4 – Ascertain the *Milestones*

Step 5 – Assign the *Activities*

Step 6 – Develop the *Reporting Requirements*

Step 7 – Select the type of *Evaluations*

Step 8 – Assimilate the *Project Essentials*

Below is an example of our Organizational Product Map:

I'm sure you've all heard the catchy phrase "fake it till you make it." With an Organizational Product Map it doesn't have to be that way. However, I really do think all too often we set out on projects where a lot of folks are faking hoping they make it. Why? Because it takes a ton of energy to do things the right way. It takes a ton of energy to sit down with someone who doesn't have the experience you do and show them how to do something the right way. It takes a ton of energy (and courage) to hold a meeting with the entire team and go around the room asking detailed questions about the scope, who's doing what, if they understand what the requirements are, if they understand what exactly you expect. And for the leader of that meeting to risk saying "I don't know...but I'll find out," it takes both a ton of energy and good dose of humility.

And that's what it takes if you're organization is going to survive the 21st Century! A ton of energy, an equal amount of enthusiasm, a good dose of humility, a tireless effort in being the "relentless encourager," the courage to make hard decisions and an unwavering commitment to be held accountable and to hold others accountable.

At this time, I hope I have provided you a "dashboard" of models that will help you in managing and sustaining your organization. As I stated in the introduction my hope is that this will NOT become just another "trophy read" that will end up on your bookshelf, but rather a trusty guide that will help you on a day-to-day basis.

Another tool I would like to offer is the Training Guide that goes along with this book. If you really do sense the material that was presented could be of value, I would highly recommend you purchase the Training Guide and take your team through the Training Guide while having them read the book.

In the final section of the book, we are going to briefly talk about leadership and then in the final chapter tie everything together. In our chapter on leadership we'll look at two very different, yet effective means of motivation: intrinsic and extrinsic. My intention is to provide, perhaps, a different angle on how leadership can be applied.

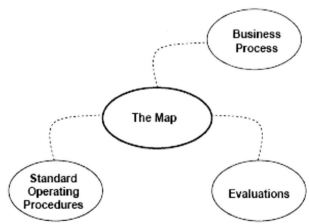

Part 5

Leadership

Leadership Overall

76%

Intrinsic

89%

Extrinsic

82%

Modeling

56%

CHAPTER FOURTEEN

Intrinsic & Extrinsic

Motivation

"There are two types of people--those who come into a room and say, 'Well, here I am!' and those who come in and say, 'Ah, there you are.'"

- Frederick L. Collins

My desire here is not to compete with those who have spent their entire professional life writing on leadership. If you're looking for an in depth study on leadership, there are a host of great resources out there. I intend only to share my view of what characteristic traits typify great leaders, as well as intrinsically challenge the reader.

I believe a quick definition of *intrinsic* and *extrinsic* may be of some help to those not familiar with these terms.

The word *intrinsic*, according to Webster's Dictionary, means *belonging to the essential nature or constitution of a thing.* So, if we are going to lead an individual or a group of individuals through intrinsic motivation, we must appeal the very constitution of their make-up. We must attempt to reach into the very core of their being to challenge and encourage them to look beyond the superficial gratification of the "now," and move them toward owning and believing that what they do today has a dramatic effect on posterity (i.e. what they leave to future generations). Another way of saying this is, get your folks to work for something bigger than themselves. If anyone understood this it was George Washington. Space and time here prohibit me from providing his farewell address, so please take the time and go read what America's first General, Commander-in-Chief and President had to say as he was leaving office. Suffice it to say that he was appealing to the very intrinsic values of the American people.

The word *extrinsic,* also according to Webster's Dictionary, simply means *not forming part of or belonging to a thing – originating from or on the outside.* So when one motivates extrinsically, he or she is offering a tangible external recompense for what someone has either earned, or giving benevolently unearned benefits. This is, in fact, a very effective way to motivate and lead, but to offer extrinsic rewards as the *only* form of motivation will result in producing intrinsically emaciated souls, who neither choose nor desire anything but self-gratification and entitlements; who, in the words of Theodore Roosevelt, will never "know victory nor defeat."

You may recall, in Chapter 2, I made the statement that if organizations are going to stand the test of time, amid the challenges that await us in the 21st century, we must begin to cultivate and water the internal organizational soil to allow individuals to be intrinsically motivated. I went on to say that we cannot *only* be extrinsically motivated through compensation, but must also be intrinsically motivated by the virtue of work itself. As I write this, I cannot help but recall the words of John Ruskin, a nineteenth century poet and social critic:

"When we build, let us think that we build forever. Let it not be for present delight nor for present use alone. Let it be such work as our descendants will thank us for; and let us think, as we lay stone on stone, that a time is to come when those stones will be held sacred because our hands have touched them, and that men

will say, as they look upon the labor and wrought substance of them, "See! This our father did for us."

What I believe he is saying is that our work must become the very fingerprint of our character. Remember the Proverb I quoted in Chapter 6: "One who is slack in his work is brother to one who destroys". Oh, how true it is! Those who simply approach each day with a complacent attitude, content with "just getting by" will be the ones in the 21st century who will be standing in line waiting for their entitlements. And those who employ them will be the very organizations that will be unable to stand the test of time.

As a leader, you must be the one who "sifts the wheat from the chaff." You must be the one who not only finds those with a "can do" attitude, but also the one who develops those around you to become leaders themselves.

Remember the words of Winston Churchill: "... *never give in, never give in, never, never, never, never-in nothing, great or small, large or petty - never give in except to convictions of honour and good sense.*"

My question to you is, are you ready to take the leadership challenge in the 21st century? Are you ready to decide from this day forward that you will be the "relentless encourager" on your team? Do you have the courage it takes to surround yourself with folks who value good character and a good work ethic, and openly say to them, "From this day forward I want you to hold me accountable for everything I do; both personally and professionally" – and live by it?

I'm sure you've heard the phrase *attitude reflects leadership.* Are you committed to reflecting a good attitude and good character within your organization? Are you committed to stop gossiping, complaining and arguing, and have the courage to inspire and encourage?

G.K. Beale said, "We resemble what we revere; to our ruin or our restoration." If that is true, do you revere the *status quo* more than you revere excellence? Do you revere eroding someone's character through gossip more than you do *not* saying anything at all? Do you revere being a cynic more than you do a problem solver? What exactly do you revere?

Do you revere reputation more than character? Are you afraid that if you walk into work on Monday with your mind set on becoming a different individual than you have been in the past that your comrades might ridicule you?

Consider for a moment this poem by William Hersey Davis:

The circumstances amid which you live determine your reputation;
the truth you believe determines your character.

Reputation is what you are supposed to be;
character is what you are.

Reputation is the photograph;
character is the face.

Reputation comes over one from without;
character grows up from within.

Reputation is what you have when you come to a new community;
character is what you have when you go away.

Your reputation is learned in an hour;
your character does not come to light for a year.

Reputation is made in a moment;
character is built in a lifetime.

Reputation grows like a mushroom;
character grows like the oak.

A single newspaper report gives you your reputation;
a life of toil gives you your character.

Reputation makes you rich or makes you poor;
character makes you happy or makes you miserable.

Reputation is what men say about you on your tombstone;
character is what angels say about you before the throne of God.

So what do you revere? These are tough questions that I hope will make you stop and think. I don't think our culture does that much anymore – that is, stop and…. think. We don't think about the importance of good character. What we think about is what we are bombarded with on every news website, TV program and newspaper headline we read – people failing at representing good character. From the top politicians on both sides of the isle to junior high school aged kids murdering their teachers. From Wall Street executives swindling millions and billions from honest hard working people to school teachers having affairs with students half their age. If Peter Drucker was right when he saw business as "society's change agent," then we – yes, you and I - have a lot of work to do; starting right where we are within our own organizations.

Perhaps you pose the challenge, "Okay, show me someone who has been able to effectively do this and have it stand the test of time." Well, there are many of them, and most of the folks I have either quoted or referenced in this book are great examples.

Another good example and perhaps the greatest example in history of melding both intrinsic and extrinsic motivation can be found in Jesus' Sermon on the Mount. And no, this is not a "bait and switch" to "convert" you to a particular religious system or way of thought. I am simply citing categorically the most widely circulated book in the history of mankind that happens to contain, arguably, the most popular sermon ever given.

He opens by intrinsically *inspiring* his audience with the beatitudes. He then goes on to explain that our good will never be good enough - but he doesn't exasperate his listeners. No, he then offers forgiveness to his followers, as he knows perfection in and of ourselves is not possible. In fact, he even scolds the perfectionists. He then *encourages* his listeners extrinsically – promising tangible external rewards to those who pursue perfection in humility and selflessness; but he doesn't stop there either. He then *challenges* his audience to get their priorities straight first, then vigorously pursue what we are called to do; and not by "leaning on our shovels while praying for a hole," but rather by "asking...seeking...and knocking." Being *diligent*! Remember who the father of execution is? Diligence.

And there are many other great examples all around us – just look for them. As I sit here writing this very chapter, I think of several folks, both men and women, who I have worked with over the years and am actually working with now. You know the ones when you walk in or see them after an extended period of time; they are genuinely glad to see you and actually greet you with a smile and a word of encouragement.

A few in particular are young ladies with a very difficult job on very difficult construction projects. No, you won't find their titles with any alphabets behind them. And, no, they aren't on the "Executive Team" either. They sit at the front desk in a large construction trailer with a host of different responsibilities and tasks that, quite frankly, if not completed would disrupt the flow of the job with disastrous effects. They have a job that many of us would probably go crazy in trying to manage, yet day after day, they do it with a smile. They greet you when you come in, and send you out with, "Have a great day." Their e-mail correspondence is always "cheery" – in a job and at a time when "cheery" isn't so popular. And, yes, they are cheery in spite of the fact a few "Snotty Pants" work there and a ton of grumpy construction guys who come in and out. Regardless, they perform their job with tireless enthusiasm and a great attitude.

No matter where you are, what title you bear, what role you play at work or at home, you're a leader. Let's take a moment to compare and contrast what leaders do and what they don't do, both intrinsically and extrinsically:

Intrinsically

(belonging to the essential nature or constitution of a thing)

LEADERS DO...	LEADERS DON'T...
ENCOURAGE EMBOLDEN	DISCOURAGE
INSPIRE AROUSE INFLUENCE	INTIMIDATE
EXHORT URGE	EMBITTER
ADMONISH CAUTION	FLATTER
CORRECT MAKE RIGHT	IGNORE
REBUKE REPRIMAND	EXASPERATE
RESTORE MEND	DESTROY

Extrinsically

(originating from or on the outside)

LEADERS DO...	LEADERS DON'T...
SYNTHESIZE COMBINE	BREAK DOWN
ORGANIZE CREATE	CONFUSE
INSTRUCT MENTOR	ABANDON
TRAIN EDUCATE	MISLEAD
APPLY EMPLOY	WITHHOLD
DEPLOY ENABLE	RETREAT

I would ask that you just take a moment to reread these leadership characteristic traits and take a short inventory of how you are doing. If you want an honest opinion of how you are doing, because we tend to think we are better than we actually are (at least I do, just ask my wife), go to our website and download our Leadership Evaluation. Give it to your co-workers or family and ask them to score you on each of these traits. You may be shocked – hopefully, in a good way. Either way, low score or high, it's still good. If you receive low scores, then you know what you need work on. If you receive high scores, keep doing what you're doing.

I have a word of caution for the reader: Beware of the IPAC's! Those are the *indifferent, pessimistic, apathetic, cynics* who somehow find their way into just about every organization. If you have them, encourage them to change and try to restore them gently. If they don't respond over time, get rid of them! Their attitudes and the long term effects they have on an organization are catastrophic.

In the words of Forest Gump, "That's all I have to say about that." Those who know me know that's not true, but that's where we'll stop for now.

In the next chapter we're going to tie everything together and review what we've learned. As a high school teacher over 20 years ago I was told to "tell'em what you're going to teach'em, teach'em and then tell'em what you taught'em". So that's what we'll do in Chapter 15 – the final chapter.

CHAPTER FIFTEEN

Tying It All Together

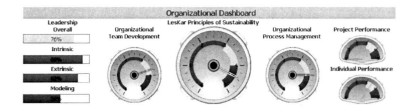

"All roads lead to Rome; which is one reason why many people never get there."

– G.K. Chesterton

Most of you can probably recall the exchange between Alice and the Cheshire Cat in Walt Disney's version of Lewis Carroll's *Alice in Wonderland*:

"'Would you tell me, please, which way I ought to go from here?' said Alice 'That depends a good deal on where you want to get to,' said the Cat. 'I don't much care where,' said Alice. 'Then it doesn't matter which way you go,' said the Cat. '--so long as I get *somewhere*,' Alice added. 'Oh, you're sure to do that,' said the Cat."

I cannot stress to you enough the importance of providing *clear direction,* a *cogent plan* and *effective means* – knowing what done looks like. Care about what you are doing. The Cheshire Cat nailed it – if you don't know or care *where* you are going, it doesn't matter how you get there. As I stated at the opening of this book, if you aim at nothing, you'll hit it every time.

One of the goals of this book was to give the reader some tangible tools that speak directly to the three component parts of any organization: the people, the processes and the products. What I have attempted to do is provide you a 'dashboard' of three very simple models, the means of creating a very simple roadmap to serve as your Organizational Compass, and a few simple evaluation forms that you can download from our website that will assist you in effectively leading your organization into the 21st century.

First and foremost, you must have an organizational model that will not only sustain your organization but challenge every individual within the organization. We called this model our Principles of Sustainability and defined it as follows: *the ability for a group of persons organized for some end of work to endure the internal and external pressures of a culture, through change and innovation, as they endeavor through their own peculiar processes to deliver their specific products.*

LesKar Principles of Sustainability

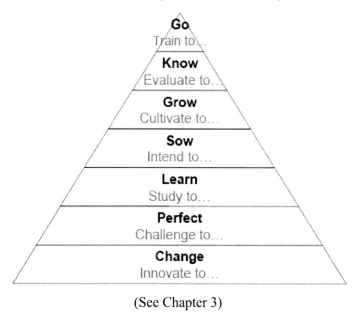

(See Chapter 3)

Implementation is the key here. Refer also to Chapter 4 for the implementation process.

Part 2 of the book dealt with Organizational Team Development. We defined Organizational Team Development as: *the exercise of transforming a committed group of individuals into a cohesive unit.*

Expanding on Patrick Lencioni's model from his book *The Five Dysfunctions of a Team*, we looked at each of the stages necessary in building a cohesive team that gets results.

Organizational Team Development

Results
Focus

Accountability
Gracious

Commit
Likeminded

Conflict
Constructive

Trust
Communication

(See Chapter 7)

Part 3 of the book discussed Organizational Process Management. Why are you doing what you are doing? Is what you are doing working? Is there room for improvement? This model, too, is intended to be used in all aspects of your organization.

You may recall our definition for Organizational Process Management: *the active effort of refining a series of rudimentary steps required to deliver a specified product or service*

Organizational Process Management

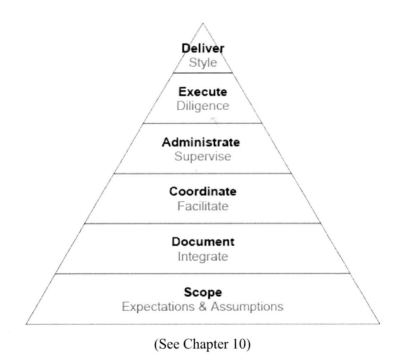

(See Chapter 10)

In Chapter 10 we briefly discussed distilling all of the information gathered from your Organizational Process Management (OPM) meeting into one document. We call it our "Work Plan." The purpose of this document is simple: get all of the pertinent information gleaned from the OPM meeting down on paper and distributed to the team in an effort to get everyone "marching to the same sheet of music."

Our 'Work Plan' Table of Contents looks like this:

Scope Summary Overview
  Scope Additions &/or Deletions
Project Goals & Objectives
  Objectives (effort needed to achieve each goal)
Role Identification
  Assign Responsibilities
Reporting Requirements
  Types of Reporting
  Frequency of Reporting
Communication Requirements
  e-mails (i.e. distribution, protocol)
  Reports (i.e. e-mailed, mailed, hand delivered)
  Design/RFI's/Submittals/System Req's, et al
Issues/Concerns/Recommendations
  Outstanding items to be clarified
Schedule
  Important Milestones
Conclusion

This is the basic outline we use in our organization. It obviously can be added to or reduced, but our encouragement to you is to have a Work Plan for every major component part of your organization or project. We often do them for special projects within a project as well.

What a Work Plan looks like will vary from organization to organization, but I would add a word of caution: Don't make your Work Plans an arduous process. In other words, don't turn them into some kind of massive tome in philosophy. At the same time, an entire Work Plan should not fit onto a single "sticky note."

Our rule of thumb: short, clear, cogent, and informative.

Last in the line up of functional tools needed for Organizational Sustainability, in Part 4 we provided the reader the means for creating an Organizational Product Map.

We defined Organizational Product Mapping as: *a graphical representation of the various phases and stages of a project.* Remember, this also serves as the portal through which members of your organization can enter your Standard Operating Procedures.

Organizational Product Mapping

These comprise the five step approach to Organizational Sustainability.

LesKar Organizational Sustainability Models

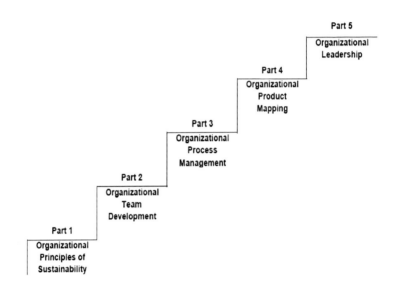

When you begin to implement and apply all of the principles discussed in this book, I predict you will begin to see the anesthetic fog of mediocrity beginning to lift. I also hope you'll discover the suffocating pressure of entitlement thinking has vanished. And lastly, I hope you begin to hear a deep sound of aspiration from those around you, who, perhaps for the first time in their lives, begin to experience the freedom of breathing and working for something bigger than themselves.

As we close, I hope you will go to our website and take advantage of the online tools available to you: LesKar Organizational Dashboard, Implementation & Training Manual, Product Mapping tools, Evaluation forms, LesKar Pocket Principles and other goods all ready to be downloaded.

I've enjoyed sharing these ideas and tools with you and would ask, in the spirit of practicing what I preach, that you e-mail me any comments or questions you may have about the book.

The organizational squid must be tamed.

Lead well!

erikpeterson@leskar.com

I'm certain most of you reading this book have all flown on a commercial airline. You make your way down the tarmac preoccupied with the person in front of you or what seat you'll be sitting in or perhaps something all together different.

I would venture to say that many of you, like me, are hardly ever preoccupied with wondering if the captain has properly filed his flight plan, or whether he will make it all the way through his pre-flight checklist. Very few of us have ever worried about whether or not all of the gauges in the cockpit are functioning properly. If you're like me, you probably never give a thought to any of those things. You assume the captain and crew have checked everything out and are relying on the gauges to function correctly.

At the same time, when you board the plane and take your seat, you don't anticipate the captain will be the one who makes his way down the aisle checking to see that everyone's luggage is "properly stowed away in the overhead bin." Nor do you expect him to be the one to answer the "call button" to retrieve a pillow for the person sitting in seat 17C. And, if you're like me, you probably don't want him focused or distracted by any of these things.

No, you want him keenly focused on what he is suppose to be doing and is trained and paid to do – that is, fly the plane!

We all know someone who is trying to operate a business *without* a "dashboard" of gauges that reflect the current status of certain parts of his organization. If you are one such person, you fall among the ranks of those who are "flying by the seat of their pants."

For most organizations, the only two "gauges" they have to work with are budget and schedule (i.e. Financials and a Gantt Chart). For a pilot, that would be like having only a fuel gauge and a temperature gauge. Can you imagine boarding an aircraft where you knew the pilot only had those two gauges available to him?

Well, it no longer has to be that way for your organization. The tools are now available for you to create your own "dashboard" equipped with gauges that reflect the critical areas of any organization which were extensively discussed in this book: sustainability, team development, process management, leadership and individual performance.

In addition, if we expect the captain of an airplane to prepare and file a flight plan, shouldn't we then create what we have coined an Organizational Product Map that safely guides us to our destination?

Now that you know the theory and philosophy behind our tools, I invite you to log on to www.LesKar.com and see how you can create what we have just described in only a few minutes. It may be the first time in your life that you feel like you are truly equipped to effectively lead your organization to succeed – in spite of the circumstances you encounter.